GW00514892

LIMITATION OF LIABILITY

All reasonable precautions have been taken to ensure complete and accurate information concerning the material presented in this workbook. However, Tektra Ltd cannot be held legally responsible for any errors or omissions in printing or faulty instructions contained within this workbook. If you find any errors in this workbook, please inform Tektra Ltd. Whilst every effort is made to eradicate typing or technical mistakes, we apologise for any errors you may detect. Your feedback is both valued by us and will help us to maintain the highest possible standards.

Information within this workbook is subject to change without notice. Companies, names and data used in examples herein are fictitious unless otherwise noted.

There are no warranties, expressed or implied, including warranties of merchantability or fitness for a particular purpose, made with respect to the materials or any information provided to the user herein. Neither the author nor publisher shall be liable for any direct, indirect, special, incidental or consequential damages arising out of the use or inability to use the content of this workbook.

Screen shots reprinted by permission from Microsoft Corporation.

Introduction To Databases

Before working through this *Database* resource pack, it is important that you read the following information that has been written to offer you guidance on how to get the best out of this resource pack.

The resource pack has been divided into units. Each unit consists of a number of IT-related categories. Throughout these categories are tasks designed to help you understand how to use the computer and how the different parts of a computer work.

At your own pace, you are required to read and work through the resource pack.

The introduction section of this resource pack is mainly theory-based, but it is essential that you read through this section and understand each category. Some parts of the resource pack will be considered recap for those that have just completed the Database resource pack 1.

At key moments throughout the resource pack, you will be instructed to perform a practical assignment or task. These tasks are there to demonstrate, with a practical hands-on approach, the important theoretical aspects of the computer that might otherwise be difficult to understand merely by reading through the resource pack.

It is important that you carefully read through each category before attempting to do the tasks, as this will equip you with the knowledge you will need to answer the questions contained within each task.

Don't worry if, occasionally, you find yourself having to refer back to the section you have just read in order to complete a task. Only through reading each category and completing the accompanying tasks will you correctly learn about the principles of databases.

Consolidation exercises are also contained within each resource pack. These exercises provide a further opportunity to recap the various categories and tasks that you will have previously undertaken, whilst working through the resource pack.

By following these simple instructions and correctly using this resource pack, you will find that learning about databases will be far more enjoyable and so much easier.

Contents

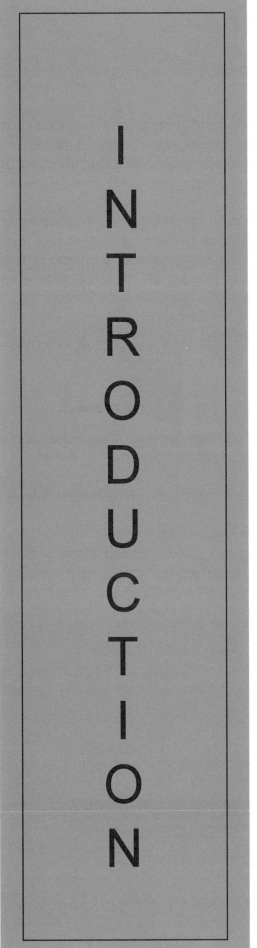

On completion of this unit, you will have learnt about and practised the following:

- **An Introduction To Access**

  - What Is A Database?
  - Basic Database Concepts
  - Access Tools
  - Why Use An Electronic Database?
  - Why Use Access?

An Introduction To Access

What Is A Database?

Most organisations, whatever their size, store paper-based information in many different places - filing cabinets, index card systems, address or telephone books, to name but a few. It can often be difficult to locate this paper-based information and this, of course, is very time-consuming.

Using a computer to store information enables you to find and update information much more quickly and easily. Just imagine that your database is the equivalent of your filing cabinet. Within a database, all information you enter is managed in a single, computerised file. The data is stored in separate storage containers (tables) which can be updated or amended as appropriate. Information can be presented in many different formats.

A database is a structured collection of related data, eg an address book or a telephone directory.

Basic Database Concepts

Before you start using Access, try and understand the following terms. If you have used a database package previously, you may recognise some of these terms.

Database file - The name given to the file when saved to disk. A file can contain numerous tables.

Table - A table, in Access, could be a complete database. As mentioned above, you can store a number of tables within one database file. However, each has to be a complete set of data about a particular subject and each will have to be given an individual name to identify it.

Record - A record is a complete set of data about one item within the table.

Field - Most tables will contain a number of fields. These are the individual headings which contain one piece of data.

Individual **Field** names

Tennis : Table

Surname	Firstname	Gender	World Ranking	Country
Hewitt	Lleyton	Male	1	Australia
Kuerten	Gustavo	Male	2	Brazil
Agassi	Andre	Male	3	USA
Kafelnikov	Yevgeny	Male	4	Russia
Ferrero	Juan Carlos	Male	5	Spain

A record ──

<u>Access Tools</u>

When working with a database, you will normally be required to do more than just key in additional data. In order to manipulate, process and present your data as useful information, you require a set of tools.

Forms

You can use a form to input, edit or view information within your database, usually record by record. Forms often resemble paper-based documents but are viewed on screen.

Select queries

These ask the questions which you might want to put to your data. Queries can be used to view, change and analyse data.

The information resulting from a select query can be sorted in ascending/descending order on a particular field, or several fields.

Action queries

These can also be questions asked about your data, but they can also result in permanent changes to your data.

Action queries available are:

        Update
        Delete
        Make-Table
        Append

Reports

Reports are an effective way of displaying information. They are designed to be printed out. You can decide on the design and layout of a report and you can use reports to present your information in a way you want. Reports also enable you to:

        Group information
        Sort information
        Calculate totals

Why Use An Electronic Database?

Electronic databases allow you to carry out the same tasks as on paper databases but with the following advantages:

- Easy to use
- Increased speed
- Ability to store large amounts of data
- Easy to input and edit data
- Easy sorting of data
- Easy search and selection of data
- Ability to format, arrange and present information as required.

Why Use Access?

A relational database contains multiple tables, each recording different areas of data. Microsoft Access is a relational database which integrates with Word, Excel and PowerPoint to make up Microsoft Office Professional.

The power of Access is that it is easy to use.

Access allows you to modify the various tables/reports/forms etc after you have entered data.

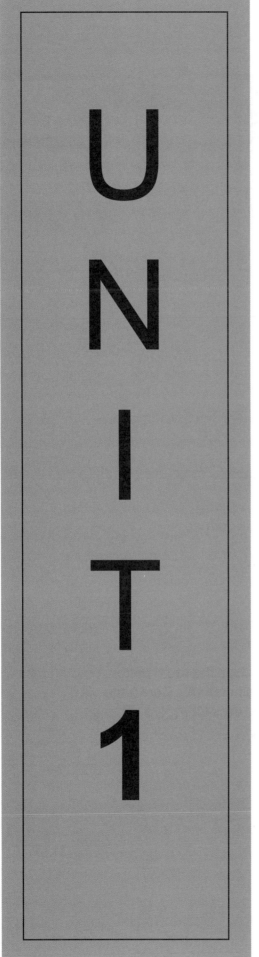

On completion of this unit, you will have learnt about and practised the following:

- **Creating Databases**

  - Starting Access
  - Creating A Database File
  - Setting Up TheTable Structure
  - Entering Field Names And Data Types

- **Defining Field Properties**

  - Field Properties
  - Text Field Properties
  - Number Field Properties
  - Currency Field Properties
  - Date/Time Field Properties
  - Switching Between Design And Datasheet View
  - Data Checking
  - Understanding Yes/No Fields
  - Descriptions
  - Further Customising Yes/No Format
  - Adjusting Field Widths

Creating Databases

Starting Access

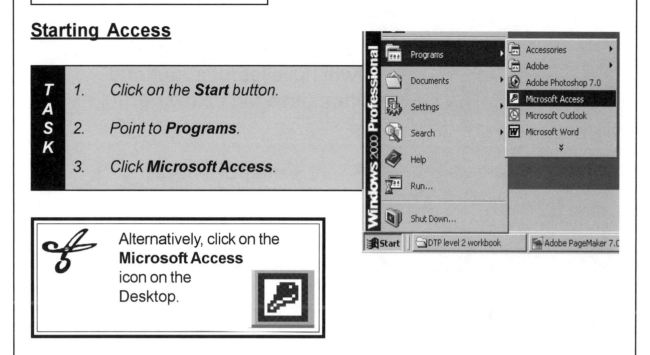

T A S K

1. *Click on the **Start** button.*

2. *Point to **Programs**.*

3. *Click **Microsoft Access**.*

Alternatively, click on the **Microsoft Access** icon on the Desktop.

Creating A Database File

Unlike word processing or spreadsheets, the database structure needs to be created before any data can be entered.

The following dialogue box appears when **Access** is opened:

Click on the radio button beside **Blank Database** and click **OK** or type **B**, then press **Enter** or click **OK**.

The **File New Database** dialogue screen will appear.

Select **3½ Floppy (A:)** from the drop-down list in the **Save in:** box.

Type the file name in the **File name** box.

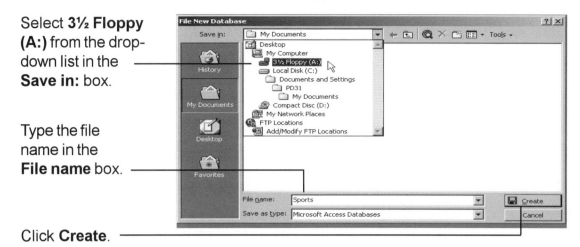

Click **Create**.

T A S K

1. *Create a new database called* **Sports***.*

You will have created a completely blank database which should appear as below:

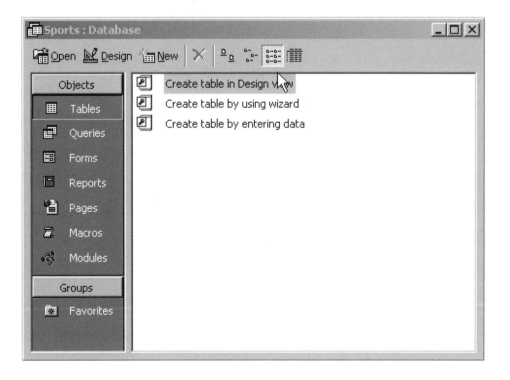

Setting Up The Table Structure

The first step in designing a database is to determine its purpose and how it is to be used. You need to know what information you want from the database. From that, you can decide what subject information you need to store in the form of **tables** and what data you want to store about the subject in the **fields**.

Determining the tables can be the trickiest step in designing a database. A table should contain information relating to one subject, therefore a database could contain many tables, each covering an individual subject. Additionally, the information entered into a table should not be duplicated in another table. This will help prevent inaccurate storing of information.

T A S K

1.   Click **Tables** from the **Objects** menu.

2.   Click **Create table in Design view**.

3.   Press **Enter**.

A blank table design will appear similar to that shown below:

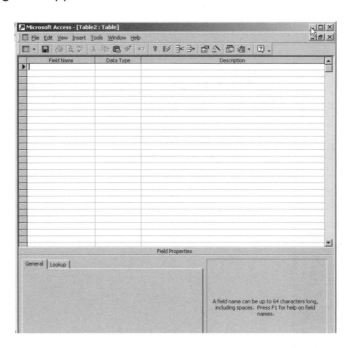

Entering Field Names And Data Types

Each field in a table contains a piece of information about the table's subject. When deciding on the fields for a table, you need to bear in mind that the information to be stored in the field should relate directly to the subject of the table. Include all the information you need in your fields but store the information in smaller parts. For example, a person's name could be split into two fields: First Name and Surname.

When you first open Design view, the cursor will be placed in the first row of the Field Name column.

Key in the first field and press the **Tab** or **Enter** key. This will move the cursor to the next column. **Text** is the default data type.

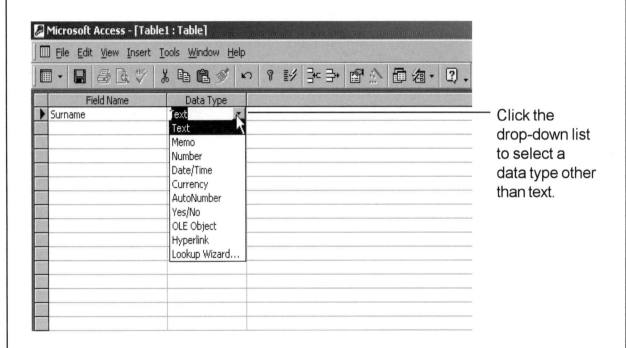

Click the drop-down list to select a data type other than text.

There are a number of different data types available for fields. It is important to select the correct data type for a field, so that only the correct type of data can be entered in the field.

Data type	Description of contents
Text	Text is the default setting and the most commonly used. Text fields can include numbers, letters and symbols or a combination, eg a car registration number P234 JKL.
Memo	Memo is similar to text although more characters can be typed in.
Number	Number fields can only include plain numbers, eg 13789. You cannot use dates, currency or text.
Date/Time	Date/Time fields can include either a date or a time, eg 23/03/1999 or 23:24.
Currency	Currency fields contain numbers formatted as money. If you enter 20, Access displays £20.00.
AutoNumber	As records are entered, they will be numbered automatically. AutoNumber must be selected when designing the initial database and cannot be added once the database already contains data.
Yes/No	A logical field which can contain one of only two values, eg Yes/No, True/False, On/Off.
OLE Object	Object linking and embedding is mainly used to link a large graphic or Internet movie. When selected, it jumps to the linked graphic or movie.
Hyperlink	Links a field to an Internet site, eg a company Internet address would be typed in the field. When the field is selected, the Internet source is opened.

TASK

1. Create a new table in the **Sports** database.

2. In the Table Design view enter the following **Field Names** and **Data Types**.

Field Name	Data Type
Surname	Text
First Name	Text
Gender	Yes/No
World Ranking	Number
Country	Text
Points	Number
DOB	Date/Time

3. Do not save or close the table.

When you have done any design work, it's up to you to save it. You will be carrying out a number of tasks on this table and it's good practise to save after each task. If you try leaving Design view without saving, Access will prompt you to save.

T A S K	1.	Click on the **Save** button on the toolbar.
	2.	Type **ABC Tennis Table** as the name for the table (where **ABC** is replaced by your initials).
	3.	Click **OK** to confirm.
		*When prompted to create a primary key, say **No**. Primary keys are explained in unit 2.*

Defining Field Properties

Field Properties

Each field has a set of properties that you use to customise how a field's data is stored, handled or displayed. For example, you can control the maximum number of characters that can be entered into a **text** field by setting its **Field Size** property. You set field properties in Table Design view by selecting the field in the upper portion of the window and then selecting the desired property in the lower portion of the window.

The properties that are available for each field are determined by the data type you select for the field.

Select the field

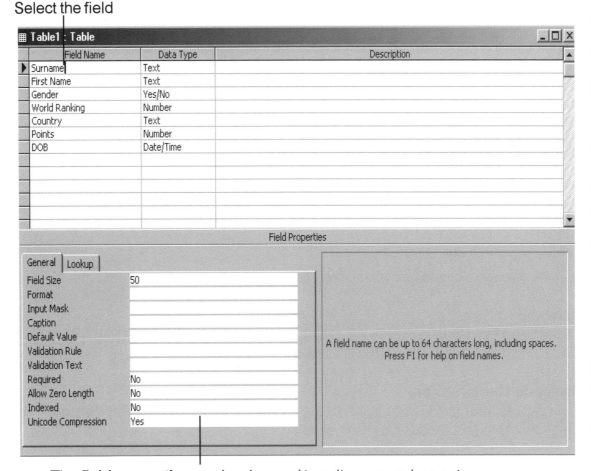

The **field properties** can be changed to suit your requirements.

Text Field Properties

Field Size
The default value is 50. This figure should be amended to allow for the longest entry into that field. The maximum that can be set is 255.

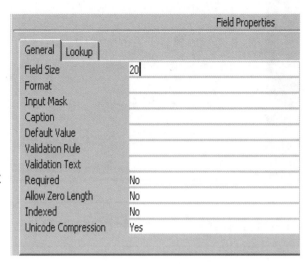

Format
Allows you to create custom formats for text by using symbols, eg
<   force all characters to lowercase
>   force all characters to uppercase.

Input Mask
An input mask allows you to control how data will look when entered in a field. For example a postcode may have letter, letter, number, space, number, letter, letter.

Caption
Text typed in the caption will be displayed as the column heading instead of the field name.

Default value
The value typed in the default box will be automatically entered into each new record. You can change it if necessary.

Validation Rule
Limits data that can be entered, for example if you enter **Not "future"** as the validation rule, when the word **"future"** is keyed into the field, an error message will appear and an alternative must be entered.

Validation Text
Your own personalised error message can be created by typing in this field. The message will be displayed if the validation rule has been broken.

Required
If this is set to **Yes**, then an entry must be made into that field and it cannot contain a null value.

Allow Zero Length
Enables you to indicate that you know there may be no value in the field.

Indexed
Selecting **Yes - No Duplicates** will prohibit duplicate values in a field.
Selecting **Yes - Duplicates OK** will allow duplicate values in a field.

Unicode Compression
The default value for Unicode compression is **Yes**. This controls the way that text is stored and compressed in Access and can save disk storage space.

T	1.	*Change the **Field Properties** for the **Text** fields to **20** to give enough character spaces for the relevant data to be added.*
A		
S		*Save your work but leave Design view open.*
K		

Number Field Properties

For **number** fields, the **Field Properties** section will appear as follows:

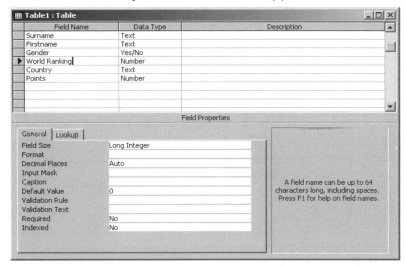

Upon selecting the **Field Size** box, a drop-down arrow appears. When clicked, it displays a list of the different field sizes available for the storage of numeric data:

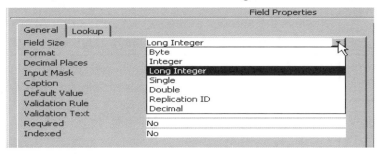

The options available include:

Byte	Stores whole numbers from 0 to 255 (no decimal places)
Integer	Stores whole numbers (no decimal places) from -32,768 to 32,767
Long Integer	Stores whole numbers (no decimal places) from -2,147,483,648 to 2,147,483,647
Single	Stores numbers (allows decimal places) from -3.402823E38 to -1.401298 for negative values and from 1.401298E-45 to 3,402823E48 for positive values.
Double	Stores numbers (allows decimal places) from -1.79769313486231E308 to -4.94065645841247E-324 for negative values and from 1.79769313486231E308 to 4.94065645841247E-324 for positive values.
Replication ID	Globally Unique Identifier, used to identify replicas.
Decimal	Stores numbers to 28 decimal places from $-10^{28} -1$ to $10^{28} -1$ (.mdb)

T
A   *Your table needs to show a World Ranking of 1 to 20 and Points covering a*
S   *range of 0 to 5000.*
K

1.   *Select suitable field sizes for the World Ranking and Points fields in your table.*

Save your work but leave Design view open.

Upon selecting the **Format** box, a drop-down arrow appears. When clicked, this displays a list of the different options for the formatting of numeric fields.

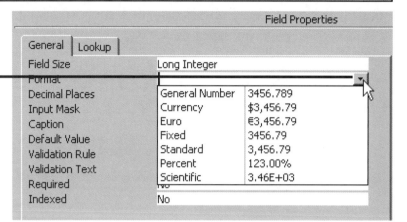

The options available include:

General Number	Displays the number as it is keyed in however it will drop leading zeros eg **03** typed in will be displayed as **3**. If you're using a field size which can allow decimals, it will also drop trailing zeros beyond the decimal point. Eg **6.30** will appear as **6.3**.
Currency	Displays the number preceded with a £ sign. Also separates thousands with a comma and has a default of two decimal places.
Euro	Displays the number preceded with a Euro sign. Also separates thousands with a comma and has a default of two decimal places.
Fixed	Most useful for fixing decimal places so as not to lose the trailing zeros.
Standard	Separates thousands with a comma and has a default setting of two decimal places.
Percent	Multiplies the value by 100 and attaches a percent sign (%) with a default setting of two decimal places.
Scientific	Converts the entered number to scientific notation.

The **Decimal Places** property allows you to specify the number of digits to the right of the decimal separator. It will allow you to store up to 15 digits.

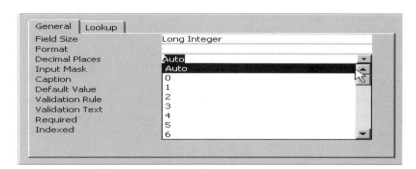

1.   Select a suitable **Number Format** for the **Point** field, to include a thousand separator.

2.   Set the required number of decimal places.

Save your work but leave Design view open.

Currency Field Properties

When **Currency** data type has been selected, the **Format** box automatically shows **Currency**.

The format property automatically applies two decimal places to your numbers. If you want any other number of decimal places (ie no decimal places), then you should click in the **Decimal Places** drop-down box and select the value you require.

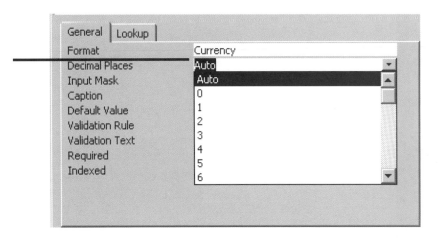

Date/Time Field Properties

Upon selecting the Format property box, a drop-down arrow appears. When clicked, this displays a list of the different formats for presenting your dates and times.

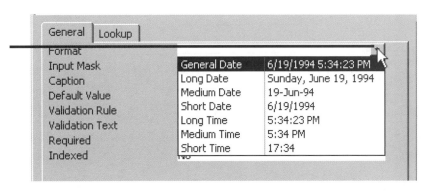

1.   Set the relevant Date/Time format to display the **DOB** as a **Short Date**.

Do not close or save the table.

The **Yes/No** field properties will be covered later on.

Switching Between Design And Datasheet View

Switching between views may be required to help sharpen the design. When creating queries, forms or reports, switching between views will be useful in improving the end result.

The **View** button is known as a toggle button. When your table is displayed in Design view, only the button to switch to Datasheet view is displayed, and vice versa.

The view buttons appear on the toolbar as:

Go to Design view   Go to Datasheet view

TASK

1. Switch to the Datasheet view and enter the following records into the **ABC Tennis Table**. No records are yet required for the **Gender** field.

Surname	First Name	Gender	World Ranking	Country	Points	DOB
Hewitt	Lleyton	☐	1	Australia	4,365	24/02/1981
Kuerten	Gustavo	☐	2	Brazil	3,855	10/09/1976
Agassi	Andre	☐	3	USA	3,520	29/04/1970
Kafelnikov	Yevgeny	☐	4	Russia	3,145	18/02/1974
Ferrero	Juan Carlos	☐	5	Spain	3,040	12/02/1980
Grosjean	Sebastien	☐	6	France	2,865	29/05/1978
Rafter	Pat	☐	7	Australia	2,785	28/12/1972
Haas	Tommy	☐	8	Germany	2,285	03/03/1978
Henman	Tim	☐	9	Britain	2,215	06/09/1974
Sampras	Pete	☐	10	USA	1,940	02/08/1971
Williams	Venus	☐	1	USA	4,790	17/06/1980
Capriati	Jennifer	☐	2	USA	4,684	29/03/1976
Davenport	Lindsay	☐	3	USA	3,862	08/06/1976
Clijsters	Kim	☐	4	Belgium	3,698	08/06/1983
Hingis	Martina	☐	5	Switerzland	3,558	30/09/1980
Henin	Justine	☐	6	Belgium	2,987	01/06/1982
Seles	Monica	☐	7	USA	2,979	18/02/1973
Dokic	Jelena	☐	8	Yugoslavia	2,974	12/04/1983
Williams	Serena	☐	9	USA	2,875	26/09/1981
Mauresmo	Amelie	☐	10	France	2,651	05/07/1979

2. Make sure you have keyed in the data accurately.

3. Check that you have entered 20 records

Data Checking

It's most important to check the accuracy of your data. If, for instance, you enter the Country for some American players as **USA** and for others as **US**, you will make it very difficult to run a query to find all the American players – Access cannot recognise that these two variants mean the same thing. Even worse is a slight spelling mistake or getting a digit wrong in a number – these can make nonsense of any searching or sorting you want to do later.

In some tables, it might help to use the spell checker. That wouldn't be any use in the name fields in this table, but you could use it in the **Country** field.

**T
A
S
K**

1. *Deliberately introduce a spelling mistake in two of your country names.*

2. *Highlight the **Country** field by clicking on its field name. Then run the spellchecker either with the ABC button or by pressing the function key* ***F7.***

    This will check the entries in this field in the dictionary. Correct your mistakes.

3. *Now check all the words and numbers you have entered on the table. You might find this easiest if you print out a copy of the table.*

4. *When you're sure that the data is correct, close the table.*

Understanding Yes/No Fields

The **Yes/No** Data Type is also known as a logical data type. It enables one of two choices to be made. Yes/No value fields contain one of two values (Yes/No, True/False or On/Off).

In Table Design view, Yes/No can be selected from the **Data Type** drop-down list.

The **Format** box provides the Yes/No, True/False, and On/Off predefined formats. If you choose one of these pre-defined formats and then enter Yes, No, True, False, On or Off in the datasheet, the pre-defined format will be displayed. For example, if you enter True or On in the datasheet when the **Format** property is set to Yes/No, the value is automatically converted to Yes.

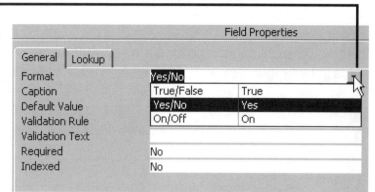

	Field Properties	
General	Lookup	
Format	Yes/No	
Caption	True/False	True
Default Value	Yes/No	Yes
Validation Rule	On/Off	On
Validation Text		
Required	No	
Indexed	No	

T A S K	1.	Open the **ABC Tennis Table** in **Design View**.
	2.	Check that the **Format** for the **Gender** field is set to **Yes/No**.

In the Datasheet view, the check box will default to an empty box. ——— ☐
This means No, False or Off.

In the Datasheet view when the check box has a tick in it, it means ——— ☑
Yes, True or On. To tick the check box, use your cursor to click the
box and a tick will appear.

The **Yes/No** data type can be formatted further. For instance, you may wish the field to display information such as:

Good	or	Bad
Achieved	or	Not Achieved
Full Time	or	Part Time

Having decided the information that you wish the Yes/No data type to display, you will need to specify this in the Properties section in Design view.

T A S K

1. *Ensure you are in Design view, select the Gender field and select the Lookup tab in the data properties section.*

2. *Click on the drop-down box and select Text Box.*

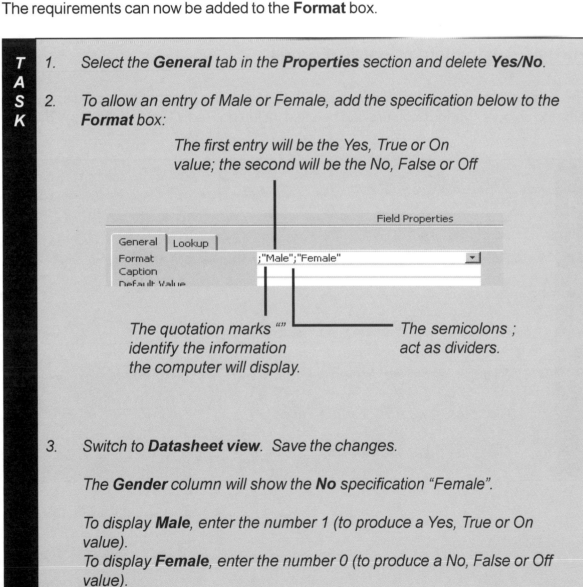

Field Properties

General | Lookup

Display Control | Check Box ▼
Check Box
Text Box
Combo Box

When you have selected **Text Box**, the information you specify will appear as text in the datasheet and not as a check box.

The requirements can now be added to the **Format** box.

T A S K

1. *Select the General tab in the Properties section and delete Yes/No.*

2. *To allow an entry of Male or Female, add the specification below to the Format box:*

The first entry will be the Yes, True or On value; the second will be the No, False or Off

Field Properties

General | Lookup

Format | ;"Male";"Female" ▼
Caption |
Default Value

*The quotation marks ""
identify the information
the computer will display.*

*The semicolons ;
act as dividers.*

3. *Switch to Datasheet view. Save the changes.*

The Gender column will show the No specification "Female".

To display Male, enter the number 1 (to produce a Yes, True or On value).
To display Female, enter the number 0 (to produce a No, False or Off value).

4. *Change the entries in the Gender field to Male for the first 10 records.*

NB **Although you have to save design work, data is automatically saved whenever you leave a record you have created or changed.**

Descriptions

Descriptions are especially useful if data required in the fields are codes. Unless a user is particularly conversant with all codes, a prompt is useful.

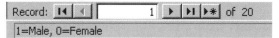

	Field Name	Data Type	Description
	Surname	Text	
	Firstname	Text	
▶	Gender	Yes/No	1=Male, 0=Female

The prompt will show up on the left of the status bar in datasheet view.

Record: |◀◀| |◀|	1	|▶| |▶◀| |▶*| of 20
1=Male, 0=Female

The above illustration indicates to the user that by adding the number one, the result displayed will be Male.

Further Customising Yes/No Format

The Yes/No format can be customised further to enable the information to be displayed in differing colours. Various colours can be used including Red, Green, Yellow and Blue.

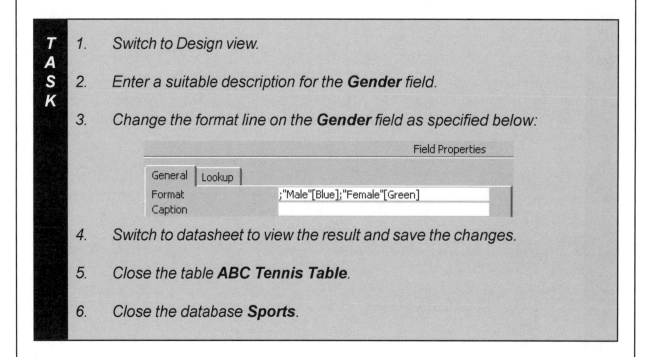

TASK

1. Switch to Design view.

2. Enter a suitable description for the **Gender** field.

3. Change the format line on the **Gender** field as specified below:

   Field Properties

   General | Lookup
   Format   ;"Male"[Blue];"Female"[Green]
   Caption

4. Switch to datasheet to view the result and save the changes.

5. Close the table **ABC Tennis Table**.

6. Close the database **Sports**.

Adjusting Field Widths

Sometimes it is not possible to see all of the data for a field when viewing a table in datasheet view. Access allows you to change the widths of the columns (fields) in order to see the data.

To change the width of a field in datasheet view, place the cursor to the right of the column heading until a double-headed arrow appears ↔. Click and drag the double-headed arrow until all the data is visible.

	Surname	First Nan	Gender	World Rar
	Hewitt	Lleyton	Male	
	Kuerten	Gustavo	Male	
	Agassi	Andre	Male	
	Kafelnikov	Yevgeny	Male	
	Ferrero	Juan Carli	Male	

ABC Tennis Table : Table

Alternatively, you may double-click on the double-headed arrow, to widen the column to fit in all of the data. If you prefer, you can select the column, and click on the **Format** menu, **Column Width** option and select **Best Fit**, to achieve the same thing.

CONSOLIDATION EXERCISE

1. *Create a new database file called **Television** on the 3½ **Floppy (A:)***

2. *Create a new table to be called **ABC Favourite Programmes Table** in Design view as outlined below (do not set a primary key):*

Field Name	Data Type
Programme Name	Text
Channel	Text
Day of Week	Text
Usual Time	Date/Time
Type of Programme	Text
Suitability	Yes/No
Repeated	Yes/No

3. *Set suitable **Properties** to ensure the data on the following page can be entered.*

4. *Adjust the field widths to view the contents.*

5. *Enter the data, shown over the page, into the **ABC Favourite Programmes Table** datasheet.*

Programme Name	Channel	Day of Week	Usual Time	Type of Programme	Suitability	Repeated
EastEnders	BBC1	Various	08:00 PM	Soap	Before Watershed	Yes
The Simpsons	BBC2	Various	06:00 PM	Cartoon	Before Watershed	Yes
Kilroy	BBC1	Various	09:00 AM	Discussion	Before Watershed	Yes
This Morning	ITV1	Various	10:30 AM	Chat	Before Watershed	No
Friends	Channel 4	Various	10:00 PM	Comedy	After Watershed	Yes
Who Wants to be a Millionaire	ITV1	Various	08:30 PM	Gameshow	Before Watershed	No
Newsnight	BBC2	Various	10:30 PM	News	After Watershed	No
Panorama	BBC1	Sunday	10:15 PM	News Investigation	After Watershed	No
Channel 4 News	Channel 4	Various	07:00 PM	News	Before Watershed	No
Home And Away	Channel 5	Various	06:00 PM	Soap	Before Watershed	No
Coronation Street	ITV1	Various	08:00 PM	Soap	Before Watershed	No
Question Time	BBC1	Thursday	10:30 PM	Political Debate	After Watershed	No
The Bill	ITV1	Thursday	08:00 PM	Drama	Before Watershed	No
Frasier	Channel 4	Friday	08:00 PM	Comedy	After Watershed	No
Crime Scene Investigation	Channel 5	Saturday	09:00 PM	Drama	After Watershed	No

5. Close the table and the **Television** database.

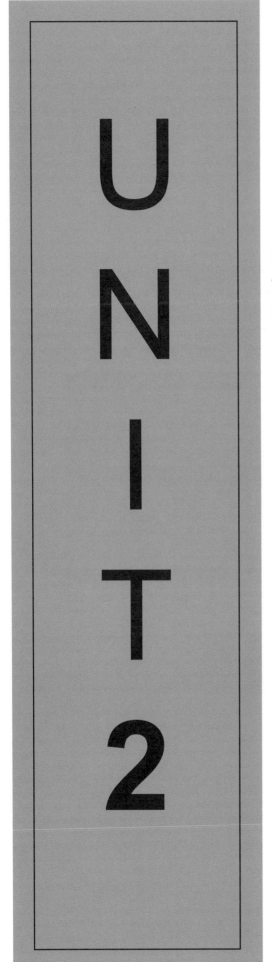

On completion of this unit, you will have learnt about and practised the following:

- **Inserting/Deleting Fields**

  · Opening The Table In Design View
  · Inserting Fields
  · Deleting A Field From A Table Design

- **Primary Keys**

  · What Is A Primary Key?
  · AutoNumber Primary Keys
  · Single-field Primary Keys
  · Setting A Primary Key (Single-field)
  · Removing A Primary Key

Inserting/Deleting Fields

Opening The Table In Design View

Click the **Tables** tab.
Click the required **Table**.
Click **Design**.

Inserting Fields

Inserting fields ensures that any data requirements missed at the design stage can be entered at a later date. However, it is always best to select all necessary fields at the earliest possible stage.

Highlight the row by clicking the **Row Selector** below where you wish to insert the new row.

Row selectors

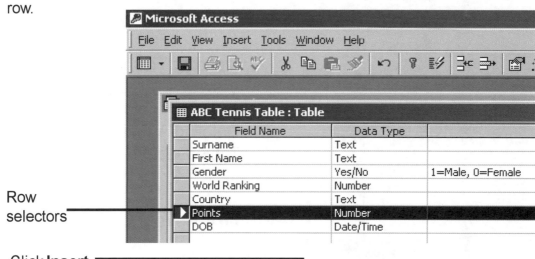

Click **Insert.**

Click **Rows.**

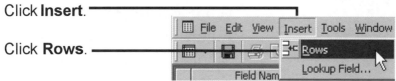

Or click on the **Insert Rows** icon on the toolbar.

A new row has now been inserted in which details can be added.

ABC Tennis Table : Table	
Field Name	Data Type
Surname	Text
First Name	Text
Gender	Yes/No
World Ranking	Number
Country	Text
Points	Number
DOB	Date/Time

T
A
S
K

1. Open the **Sports** database.

2. Open the table design for the **ABC Tennis Table**.

3. Insert a new row called **Play Hand** between **Country** and **Points** as a logical **Yes/No** data type.

4. Set the properties as **Right-Handed** for **Yes** and **Left-Handed** for **No**.

5. All the tennis players are right-handed except for Monica Seles. Make the alterations to the Play Hand field.

6. Close the table and the database.

Deleting A Field From A Table Design

Ensure that you are in the Design view of the table.

Click on the row selector beside the field that you wish to delete.

Click **Edit** and **Delete Rows**.

Or click on the icon

Rows can still be deleted if you have information stored within the table. However, a message dialogue box will ask if you wish to permanently delete the selected fields. Click **Yes** if you are sure.

You can also delete a field while in Datasheet view:

Highlight the column by clicking on the field name.

Select **Delete Column** from the **Edit** menu or on the shortcut (pop-up) menu you get if you right-click on the column.

In some ways it's safer to delete from Datasheet view because you can see the data you are deleting as well as the field name.

Primary Keys

What Is A Primary Key?

A database system such as Microsoft Access must be useful in being able to quickly find and bring together information stored in separate tables using queries, forms and reports. In order to do this, each table should include a field that uniquely identifies each record stored in the table. This information is called the **primary key** of the table. Once you designate a primary key for a table, Microsoft Access will prevent any duplicate values from being entered in the primary key fields.

When you make a field into a primary key, Access automatically indexes that field. If there are no other indexes or sorts, this index will set the sort order for the table.

The primary key provides the quickest path to locate any record when its identifying properties are known. In relational databases, relationships between tables are created through their primary keys. This is beyond the present course.

There are different kinds of primary keys that can be defined in Microsoft Access.

AutoNumber Primary Keys

An **AutoNumber** field can be set at the design stage and will automatically enter a new number as each record is added to the table. This is the simplest method to create a primary key. If you don't set a primary key before saving a newly created table, Microsoft Access will ask if you want it to create a primary key for you. If you answer **Yes**, Microsoft Access will create an **AutoNumber** primary key.

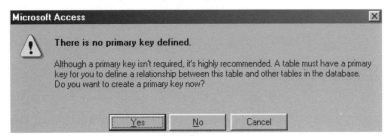

If you've already got an AutoNumber field, Access will appoint it as primary key. If not, Access will create an AutoNumber field called **ID** as primary key.

T A S K	1.	Create a new database called **Police Records** on your **3½ Floppy (A:)**		
	2.	Design your database with suitable properties according to this structure.	**Field Name**	**Data Type**	**Properties**

Field Name	Data Type	Properties
Surname	Text	25
First Name	Text	25
Street	Text	60
Town	Text	40
Postcode	Text	9
Telephone Number	Text	15
Date of Birth	Date/Time	Short Date
Crime Reported	Text	40
Date and Time Reported	Date/Time	General Date
Location	Text	25
Visit Required	Yes/No	Yes/No

> 3. Save the table as **ABC Police Reports Table** and set an **AutoNumber** primary key.

The database design view will show a new field called **ID** with a data type called **AutoNumber**.

	Field Name	Data Type	Description
🔑	ID	AutoNumber	

The datasheet view will show the field with **AutoNumber** highlighted ready for a new record to be added.

ID	Crime Ref No	Surname	First Name	Street
▶ (AutoNumber)	0			

The **New Values** property of an AutoNumber field defaults to **Increment**. This means that a new record is given the next available whole number in sequence. This is usually what you want to happen. Setting that property to **Random** makes the field select available numbers at random, not in sequence. It's hard to think of any reason why anyone would want this to happen.

The number assigned is unique to that record and cannot be used again. Even if a record is deleted, Access won't allow its AutoNumber ID to be used again by a new record.

Single-field Primary Keys

If you have a field that contains unique values such as **ID** numbers or part numbers, you can designate that field as the primary key. If the field you select as primary key does have duplicate or **Null** values, Microsoft Access won't set the primary key. Once set, the primary key will not allow duplicate data or a null value.

You can create primary keys consisting of two or more fields, but the need for them arises in database structures beyond the scope of this course.

Setting A Primary Key (Single-field)

Ensure that you are in the Design view of the table.

Click on the row selector against the field that requires the **primary key**. ────

Click on the
Primary Key ────
icon on the
toolbar.

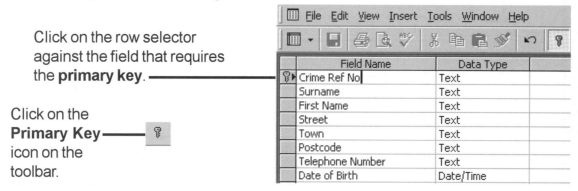

Save the changes by clicking on **Save** on the toolbar.

Note: if you create a new AutoNumber field in a table which already contains data, Access will assign values to that field for all existing records.

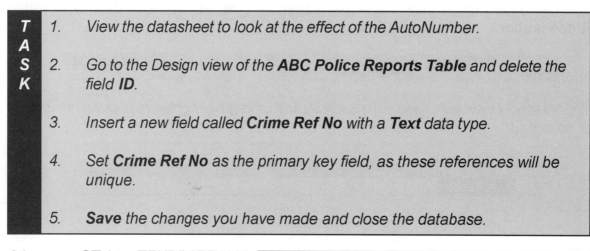

T A S K

1. *View the datasheet to look at the effect of the AutoNumber.*

2. *Go to the Design view of the **ABC Police Reports Table** and delete the field **ID**.*

3. *Insert a new field called **Crime Ref No** with a **Text** data type.*

4. *Set **Crime Ref No** as the primary key field, as these references will be unique.*

5. ***Save** the changes you have made and close the database.*

Removing A Primary Key

To remove a primary key which has been set incorrectly on a field:

First, select the **Field Name** where the primary key has been set. ——

Then click on the **Primary Key** icon.

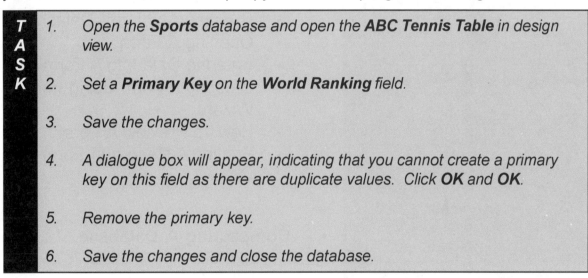

Save the changes.

In a table which already contains data, if you want an AutoNumber field to revert to an ordinary Number field, Access won't let you do it. The only way is to delete the field (and lose all data in it) and then create a new Number field with the same name. You would then need to re-enter all the data for that field. If the table is the only store of your data, you would need to make a back up copy before attempting such a change.

T A S K

1. *Open the **Sports** database and open the **ABC Tennis Table** in design view.*

2. *Set a **Primary Key** on the **World Ranking** field.*

3. *Save the changes.*

4. *A dialogue box will appear, indicating that you cannot create a primary key on this field as there are duplicate values. Click **OK** and **OK**.*

5. *Remove the primary key.*

6. *Save the changes and close the database.*

NB In an examination, you are likely to be required to produce evidence of your table design work. Access has no facility for printing Table Design view, but Windows has a **Print Screen** facility which you can use.

First, identify the **Print Screen** key on the keyboard (usually next to the **Scroll Lock**). To make a copy of the entire screen, press **Print Screen**. To make a copy only of the active window, press **Alt+Print Screen**. These actions place a bitmap picture on the Windows clipboard. You can paste this picture into various other applications. Probably the most convenient is Word.

Open Word with a blank document
Paste (**Ctrl+V**) to insert the picture
Resize picture as appropriate
Add whatever you want by way of header and footer.

If you have problems positioning the picture where you want it on the page, then try pasting it into a text box (whose border you can make transparent). You can then put the text box where you want it.

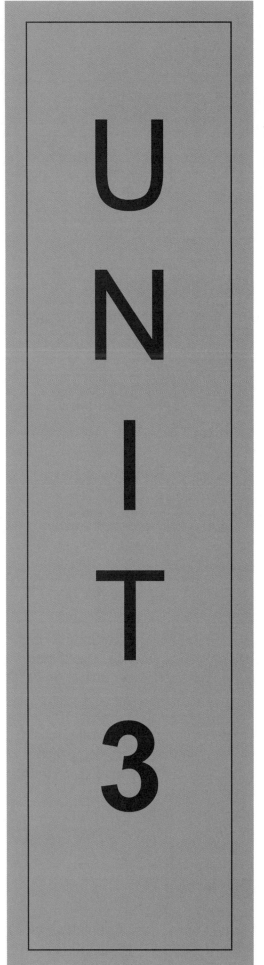

On completion of this unit, you will have learnt about and practised the following:

- **Forms**

  - Which Form To Use?
  - Creating A Form Using AutoForm
  - Creating Autoform: Columnar
  - Creating Autoform: Tabular
  - Creating Autoform: Datasheet
  - Opening A Form
  - Entering Data Into A Form
  - Creating A Form Using Form Wizard
  - How To Preview A Form
  - Printing A Record In Form View

- **Compacting A Database**

  - Why Compact A Database?
  - How To Compact A Database

Forms

Forms can be used to enter, change or view data. They are used as a more 'user-friendly' method to enter data into a database and improve the way in which data is displayed on the screen. You can create a form on your own or you can have Access create one for you, using a Form Wizard.

Which Form To Use?

There are a variety of methods which can be utilised to create a form using Microsoft Access.

With **AutoForm**, you select one information source and either columnar, tabular or datasheet layout. **AutoForm** creates a form that uses all the fields from the source selected and all the fields from its related sources.

When using a **Form Wizard**, detailed questions are asked about the information sources, fields, layout and format you want and creates a form based on your answers.

A form can be created step by step or from scratch using the Design view.

Whichever method is used, you will use similar steps to create every form.

Type of Form	Function
Design view	Design a form from scratch.
Form Wizard	Automatically creates a form based on the fields selected.
AutoForm: columnar	Creates a columnar form with all the field labels appearing in the first column and the data in the second. The form displays one record at a time.
AutoForm: tabular	Tabulates a screen full of records in tabular form with the field labels appearing at the head of each column.
AutoForm: datasheet	Similar to the tabular form, but displayed in datasheet display format.
Chart Wizard	Displays data graphically.
PivotTable Wizard	Creates a form with an Excel PivotTable - an interactive table that can summarise a large amount of data using the format and calculation methods specified by the user.

Creating A Form Using AutoForm

AutoForm creates a form that displays all fields and records in the underlying table. If the record source you select has related tables or queries, the form will also include all the fields and records from those record sources.

Creating AutoForm: Columnar

In a **Columnar Form**, each field appears on a separate line with a label to its left. Open the database and select the **Forms** tab.

Select **New** and the **New Form** dialogue box will open.

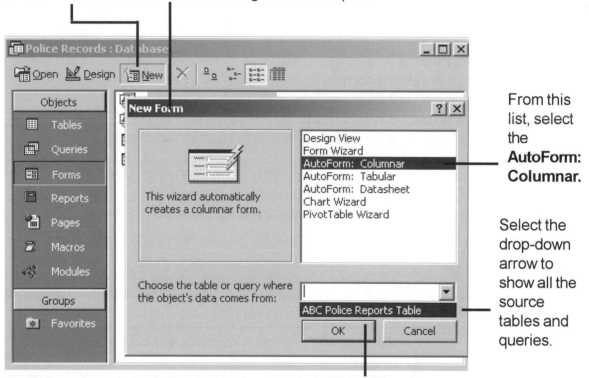

From this list, select the **AutoForm: Columnar.**

Select the drop-down arrow to show all the source tables and queries.

Once the source information has been selected, click **OK**.

T A S K		
	1.	*Open the database **Police Records**.*
	2.	*Create an **AutoForm: Columnar** based on the **ABC Police Reports Table**.*
	3.	*Save and close the form with the name **ABC Columnar Police Reports Form**.*

This is an example of a columnar form. Yours may appear differently.

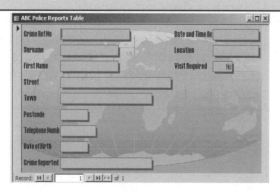

Creating AutoForm: Tabular

In a **Tabular AutoForm**, the fields in each record appear on one line, with the labels displayed once at the top of the form.

Open the database and select the **Forms** tab. Select **New** and the **New Form** dialogue box will open. From the list, select the **AutoForm: Tabular**.

Select the drop-down arrow to show all the source tables and queries. Once the source information has been selected, click **OK**.

> **T**
> **A**
> **S**
> **K**
>
> 1. Create an **AutoForm: Tabular** based on the **ABC Police Reports Table**.
>
> 2. Save and close the form with the name **ABC Tabular Police Reports Form**.

The form should appear similar to this:

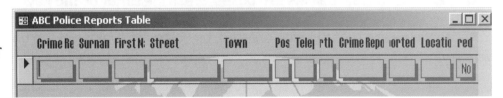

Creating AutoForm: Datasheet

A **Datasheet AutoForm** places the fields in each record in row-and-column format, with one record in each row and one field in each column. The field names appear at the top of each column.

Open the database and select the **Forms** tab. Select **New** and the **New Form** dialogue box will open. From the list, select the **AutoForm: Datasheet**.

Select the drop-down arrow to show all the source tables and queries. Once the source information has been selected, click **OK**.

> **T**
> **A**
> **S**
> **K**
>
> 1. Create an **AutoForm: Datasheet** based on the **ABC Police Reports Table**.
>
> 2. Save and close the form with the name **ABC Datasheet Police Reports Form**.

The form should appear similar to this:

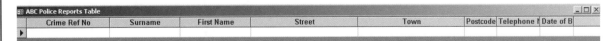

Opening A Form

To open a form:

Make sure the database file is open.

Select **Forms** from the **Objects** list. ——

Select the form to open.

Click **Open** on the toolbar or double-click on the form name.

Entering Data Into A Form

Place your cursor into the first available blank record. Type in the data into the appropriate text box. To move between the text boxes, press the **Enter** or **Tab** key.

You can view each record, once entered, by using the toolbar at the bottom of the form window.

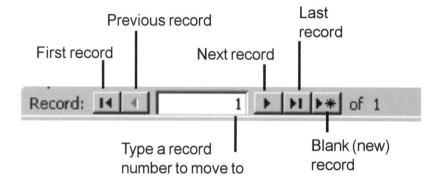

When adding new records to an existing form containing data, you will need to click on the **New Record** button.

TASK

1. In the **Police Records** database, open the **ABC Columnar Police Reports Form**.

2. Enter the records detailed on the next page into the **ABC Columnar Police Reports Form**.

TASK

Record	Crime Ref No	Surname	First Name	Street	Town	Postcode	Telephone Number
1	GT-2233-2B	Bailey	Samantha	79 Fouracre Crescent	Bath	BA5 6SE	(0118) 4568952
2	MP-7894-4M	Williams	Paula	82 Varsity Way	Bath	BA5 8SE	(0118) 4568446
3	MG-8754-2M	Dury	David	87 Park Lane	Bristol	BS11 9NE	(0117) 9213454
4	MG-8745-2M	Stone	Ann	10 High Street	Bristol	BS12 2NW	(0117) 9897637
5	CV-3215-3C	Tucker	Jason	27 Ansons Drive	Bristol	BS12 3NW	(0117) 9786129
6	BT-8999-3B	Graham	Martin	226 High Street	Bristol	BS12 8NW	(0117) 9652315
7	HB-6548-2B	Harrop	Nicholas	15 Queens Drive	Bristol	BS14 2NE	(0117) 9896541
8	CT-7788-3C	Jenkins	Barbara	68 Prince Street	Bristol	BS14 3NE	(0117) 9856196
9	HB-6599-2B	Jones	Pauline	58 Feltham Road	Bristol	BS14 6NW	(0117) 9886542
10	HB-6587-2B	Stevens	Andy	19 Maple Walk	Bristol	BS15 6SE	(0117) 9326588

Record	Date of Birth	Crime Reported	Date and Time Reported	Location	Visit Required
1	21/11/1955	Garden Furniture Stolen	01/02/2001 23:05:00	Mangotsfield	Yes
2	26/09/1967	Mobile Theft	10/10/2001 16:45:00	Blagdon	No
3	14/07/1980	Mugging	14/06/2000 18:01:00	Staplehill	Yes
4	09/06/1960	Mugging	09/04/2000 17:00:00	Staplehill	Yes
5	28/05/1969	Car Vandalised	11/05/2001 11:15:00	Thornbury	Yes
6	05/03/1979	Bike Theft	19/03/2001 10:11:00	Filton	No
7	24/10/1969	House Break-in	18/12/2001 12:00:00	Coalpit Heath	Yes
8	12/06/1975	Car Tyres Slashed	19/04/2001 23:30:00	Filton	Yes
9	04/08/1967	House Burglary	15/12/2001 03:00:00	Thornbury	Yes
10	10/10/1976	House Break-in	31/10/2001 23:20:00	Emersons Green	Yes

3. Save the table and close the database.

Creating A Form Using Form Wizard

The wizard will ask detailed questions about the record sources, fields, layout and format you want and will create a form based on your answers.

Open the database.

Select **Forms** from the **Objects** list.

Select **New**

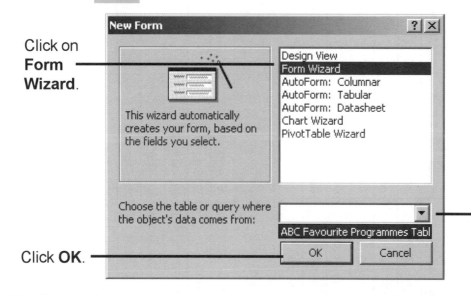

Click on **Form Wizard**.

Click on drop-down arrow and select the table from which you want to create the form.

Click **OK**.

The **Form Wizard** dialogue screen allows you to select which fields will appear on the form.

Select the table or query to use for the form.

To select specific fields, select a field and click ⟩ . The selected field will appear in the **Selected Fields** section.

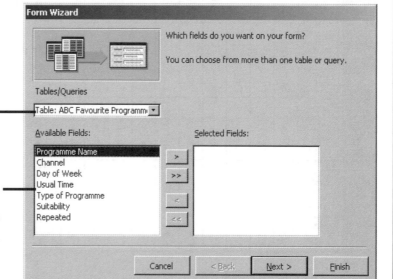

If you make a mistake, click on ⟨ and the field will move back to the left.

To select all fields from the table, click ⟩⟩ .

Once you have finished selecting fields, click **Next** to confirm your choice and move on to the next dialogue box.

T A S K

1. Open the **Television** database.

2. Select the **Form Wizard** to create a form on the **ABC Favourite Programmes Table**.

3. Select only the fields **Programme Name**, **Channel**, **Type of Programme** and **Suitability**.

The next dialogue box allows you to decide on the layout of the finished form.

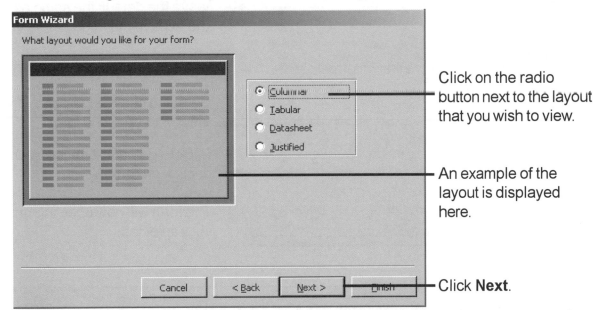

Click on the radio button next to the layout that you wish to view.

An example of the layout is displayed here.

Click **Next**.

T A S K

1. Select any one of the layouts of your own choice.

2. Click **Next**.

The next dialogue box allows you to specify the background style.

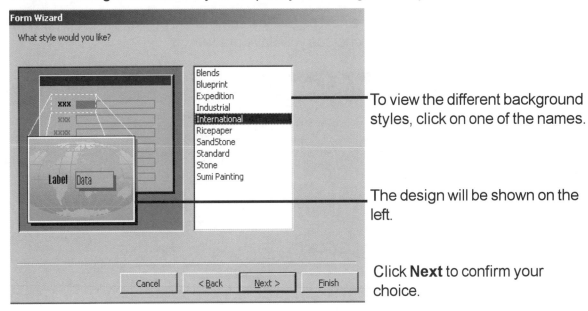

To view the different background styles, click on one of the names.

The design will be shown on the left.

Click **Next** to confirm your choice.

T A S K

1. *Select one of the background styles of your choice.*

2. *Click **Next.***

The next dialogue box allows you to give the form a name and open it.

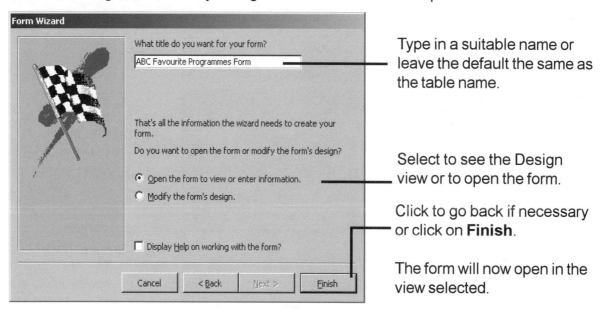

Type in a suitable name or leave the default the same as the table name.

Select to see the Design view or to open the form.

Click to go back if necessary or click on **Finish**.

The form will now open in the view selected.

T A S K

1. *Type in a suitable title for the form.*

2. *Go back to make any alternative choices.*

3. *Select to open the form and click **Finish**.*

4. *View the form and close the database.*

The following examples on this and the next page show some of the possible forms produced. Yours may differ, depending on the choices you have made.

A finished columnar form:

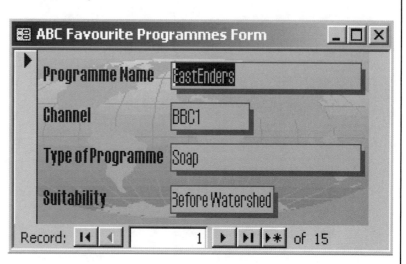

A finished tabular form:

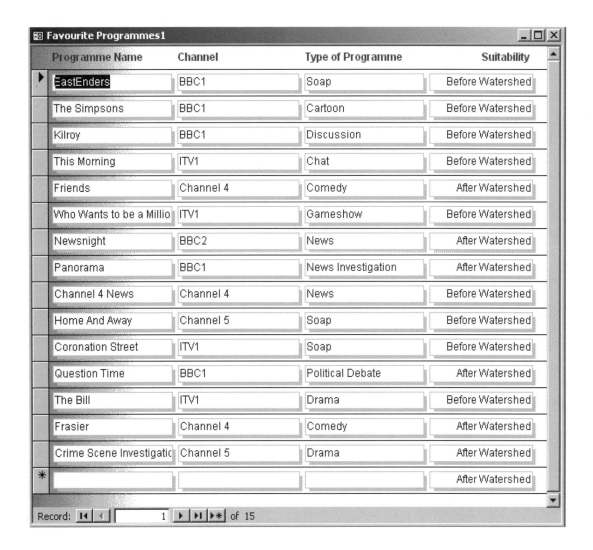

A finished justified form:

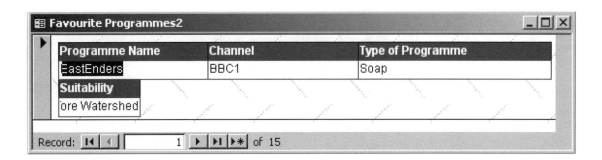

How To Preview A Form

Select **Forms** under **Objects**.

Select the form you want to preview.

Click the **Print Preview** icon 🔍 on the toolbar.

The way in which Microsoft Access displays the form in print preview depends on the view from which you preview it:

In Design view, the form appears in Form view.
In Form view, the form appears in Form view.
In Datasheet view, the form appears as a datasheet.

Printing A Record In Form View

Open the form.

Use the record selector buttons Record: |◄| |◄| [5   ] |►| |►|| |►*| of 15 to find the record required for printing.

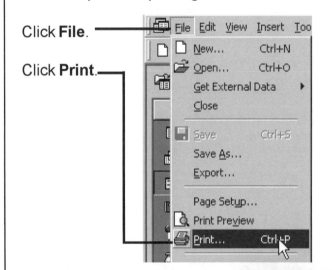

Click **File**.

Click **Print**.

Note: The **Print** 🖨 icon on the toolbar will print out all records, not just the one you want.

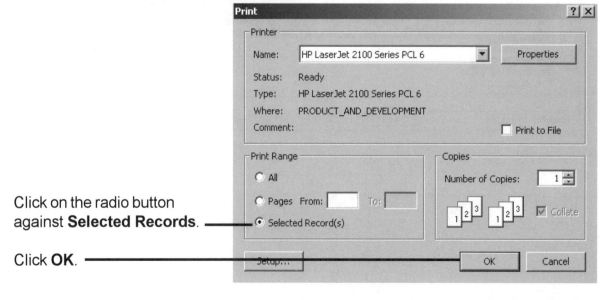

Click on the radio button against **Selected Records**.

Click **OK**.

T A S K

1. Open the **Sports** database.

2. Use the **Form Wizard** to produce a form as described below:

   The data is to come from the **ABC Tennis Table** and should include all the fields.

   The layout should be **Justified** with **Stone** used for the style.

3. Save the form with the name **ABC Tennis Justified Form**.

4. Click the **New Record** button. ▶✳

5. Add the following records to the table, using the form:

Surname	First Name	Gender	World Ranking	Country	Play Hand	Points	DOB
Safin	Marat	Male	11	Russia	Right-Handed	1,920	27/01/1980
Ivanisevic	Goran	Male	12	Croatia	Left-Handed	1,771	13/09/1971
Federer	Roger	Male	13	Switzerland	Right-Handed	1,745	08/08/1981
Roddick	Andy	Male	14	USA	Right-Handed	1,603	30/08/1982
Canas	Guillermo	Male	15	Argentina	Right-Handed	1,572	25/11/1977
Johansson	Thomas	Male	16	Sweden	Right-Handed	1,540	24/03/1975
Corretja	Alex	Male	17	Spain	Right-Handed	1,525	11/04/1974
Clement	Arnaud	Male	18	France	Right-Handed	1,475	17/12/1972
Moya	Carlos	Male	19	USA	Right-Handed	1,310	27/08/1976
Portas	Antonio	Male	20	Sapin	Right-Handed	1,220	15/11/1973
Testud	Sandrine	Female	11	France	Right-Handed	2,088	03/04/1972
Shaughnessy	Meghann	Female	12	USA	Right-Handed	1,893	13/04/1979
Farina-Elia	Silvia	Female	13	Italy	Right-Handed	1,795	27/04/1972
Dermentieva	Elena	Female	14	Russia	Right-Handed	1,658	15/10/1981
Sanchez-Vicario	Arantxa	Female	15	Spain	Right-Handed	1,548	18/12/1971
Tauziat	Nathalie	Female	16	France	Right-Handed	1,464	17/10/1967
Coetzer	Amanda	Female	17	South Africa	Right-Handed	1,451	22/10/1971
Maleeva	Magdalena	Female	18	Bulgaria	Right-Handed	1,240	01/04/1975
Raymond	Lisa	Female	19	USA	Right-Handed	1,880	10/08/1973
Tulyaganova	Iroda	Female	20	Uzbekistan	Right-Handed	1,168	07/01/1982

6. Print out the last record only in Form view.

7. Close the form and then close the database.

Compacting A Database

Why Compact A Database?

When you use an Access database, there are many occasions when data is deleted and amended. You may create queries which are deleted. Records may be updated and data removed from them. The database can become fragmented (disjointed) and use disk space inefficiently. Compacting the database optimises the performance and condenses the amount of disk space used. When compacting, the Access database makes a copy of the file and rearranges how the file is stored on your disk. In order to do this, there needs to be enough spare storage space on the disk.

Normally you would not create a database onto a floppy disk as it does not have enough memory space to hold a large amount of data. For the purposes of this resource pack, a floppy disk has been used. For the remaining units you will need to use the databases you have created, together with a further database. However, these will not fit onto your 3½ Floppy (A:) unless they are compacted. To do this we will need to move the databases temporarily into My Documents (hard drive).

How To Compact A Database

Close any open databases.

The current size of the database will appear here when in Details view.

Open **Windows Explorer**.

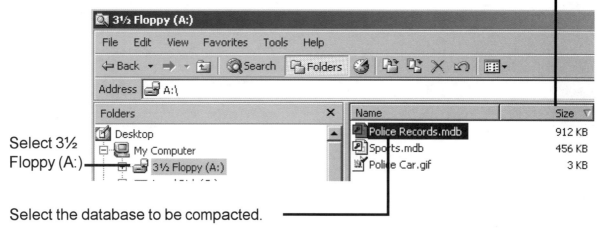

Select 3½ Floppy (A:)

Select the database to be compacted.

Click **Edit**.
Click **Cut**.

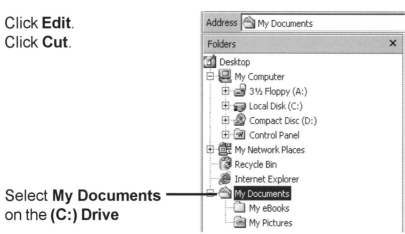

Select **My Documents** on the **(C:) Drive**

©Tektra TEKDB2RP1102

Click **Edit**.
Click **Paste** (or use the shortcut **Ctrl+V**).
Open the database which is now located in **My Documents**.

Select **Tools**.

Point to **Database Utilities**

Click **Compact and Repair Database**.

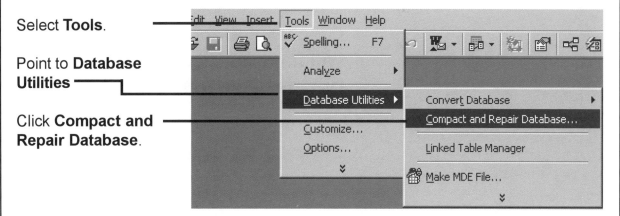

Close the database.
Click on the database.
Click **Edit**.
Click **Cut**.

Select the **3½ Floppy (A:)**

Click **Edit**.
Click **Paste**.

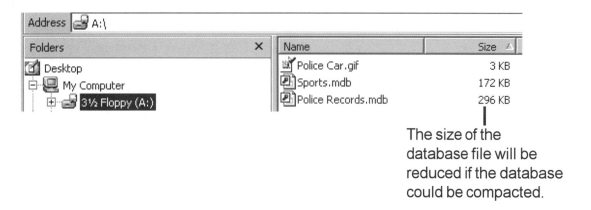

The size of the database file will be reduced if the database could be compacted.

NB The size of the database may not compact any further than its existing size.

T A S K	1.	*Move each database stored on your 3½ Floppy (A:) to My Documents.*
	2.	*Compact and repair each of the databases.*
	3.	*Move the compacted databases back onto your 3½ Floppy (A:).*
	NB	*You will need to compact your databases at various points as you work through the rest of this resource pack.*

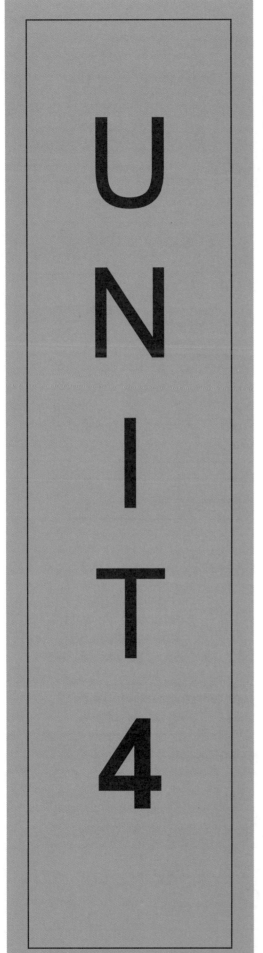

On completion of this unit, you will have learnt about and practised the following:

- **Form Modification**

  - Modifying The Form
  - Creating A Form Heading
  - Adjusting Labels And Text Boxes
  - Moving The Labels And Text Boxes Together
  - Moving The Label Box Separately From The Text Box
  - AligningControls
  - Using The Properties Organiser
  - Creating A Form In Design View
  - Adding Or Removing A Form Header/Footer Or A Page Header/Footer
  - Creating A Bound Text Box
  - Formatting Labels And Text Boxes
  - The Form And Section Selector
  - Setting The Tab Order
  - Inserting Graphics
  - Creating A Command Button

Form Modification

Modifying The Form

Modifying the form may be necessary to ensure that a pleasing format is achieved.

To modify a form:

Select the form and switch to Design view ☒ Design on the toolbar.

The screen will
appear similar to
that shown.

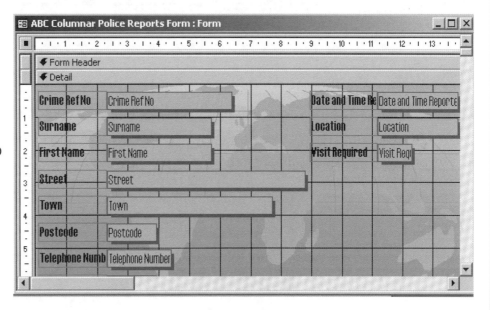

When the form is switched to Design view, a Toolbox appears. If this does not appear, click 🛠 on the toolbar. This Toolbox can be used to design a form from scratch or add to an existing form.

Select Objects		Control Wizards
Label		Text Box
Option Group		Toggle Button
Option Button		Check Box
Combo Box		List Box
Command Button		Image
Unbound Object Frame		Bound Object Frame
Page Break		Tab Control
Subform/Subreport		Line
Rectangle		More Controls

Creating A Form Heading

A form header displays information that you want to show, such as a title for the form. A form header appears at the top of the screen in Form view and at the top of the first page when printed.

Place the cursor in between the **Form Header** and **Detail** sections and a double-headed arrow will appear.

Using the double-headed arrow, click and drag down to allow space for a form heading.

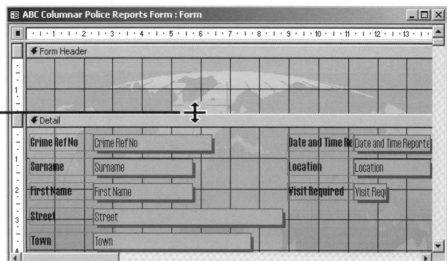

Click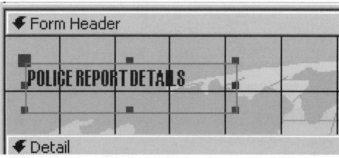

Move your cursor into the space in the form header that your cursor will have changed to show $^+\mathbf{A}$. Click and drag across and down to form a rectangle in the **Form Header** as shown and type the required heading in the space provided. Press the **Enter** key or click outside of the rectangle.

T A S K	1.	Create a space in the **Form Header** section.
	2.	Add the heading **POLICE REPORT DETAILS** in the space provided and press the **Enter** key.
	3.	Click onto the rectangle surrounding POLICE REPORT DETAILS to select the text and change the font size to **20**.
	4.	Change the font type to **Arial**.
		[If you can't see the Formatting toolbar, right-click on the menu bar and select **Formatting (Forms and Reports)**.*]*
	NB	**The heading may not fit - this will be adjusted later.**

The heading may not fit in the space provided. Clicking once onto the heading selects the heading box.

The eight square boxes surrounding the heading are known as **grab handles**. If you place your cursor over one of these, the cursor changes to a double-headed arrow. Click and drag to resize.

↕ Vertical resize   ↖ Diagonal resize

↔ Horizontal resize   ↙ Diagonal resize

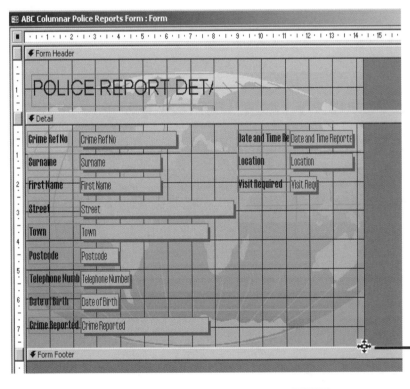

Resize the actual form by clicking on the bottom right-hand corner and dragging to ensure all staff details can be viewed.

By switching between the **Design view** 📐 ▾ and **Form view** 🔲 ▾ you can see how the form is progressing and make any changes necessary.

T A S K	1.	*Adjust the heading so that it is clearly visible when viewed in Form view.*
	2.	*Resize the form as necessary.*

Adjusting Labels And Text Boxes

Some of the field headings and/or the text box data may not fit in. These can be resized in the same way as the form heading, using the double-headed arrows.

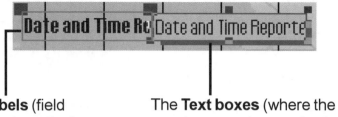

The **Labels** (field headings) are the boxes to the left.

The **Text boxes** (where the user types each record entry) are on the right.

Moving The Labels And Text Boxes Together

Click and hold once on either the label or the text box and a hand will appear.

Both boxes can be dragged to the new position. Let go when the desired position is found.

Moving The Label Box Separately From The Text Box

Click once on the box that you wish to move; a bigger square appears in the top left-hand side of the selected boxes.

Moving the pointer over the bigger square of either the label or text box will change the cursor to a pointing hand

Click and drag and the selected box only will move.

NB   The **Label** and **Text** box can overlap.

T A S K

1. Move the labels and text boxes so that the form appears similar to that shown below.

2. Change the font type for the labels and text boxes to Arial.

3. Adjust the label and text boxes so that the field headings and data are visible.

4. Save the updated form by clicking **Save**. Close the form.

Your design should be similar to the one given below:

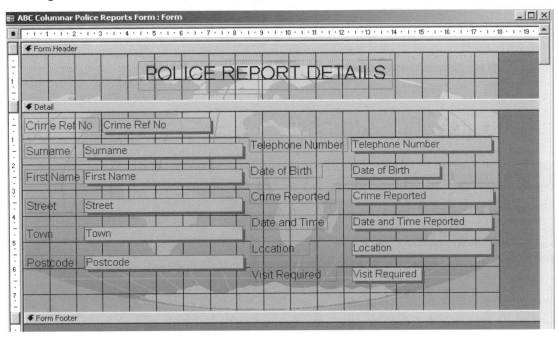

Your form should be similar to the one given below (your backgound may be different):

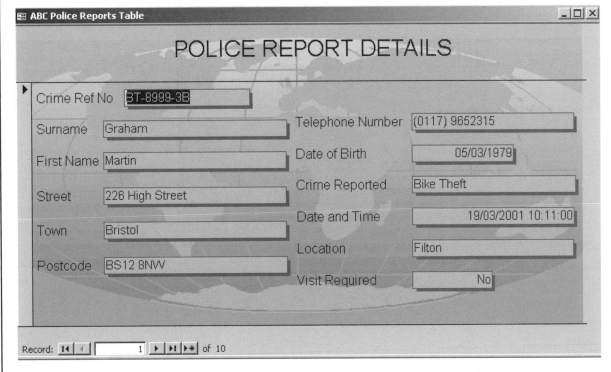

Aligning Controls

Access offers tools for aligning controls on the form. On the **Format** menu are three tools:

    Align
    Horizontal Spacing
    Vertical Spacing.

The effects which these tools offer apply to whatever group of controls you have selected. Their use is best learnt by experiment.

When your experiments go wrong, you will need the **Undo** button:

Clicking on this button allows you to undo your last action. If you click on the drop-down arrow, you can opt to undo all the actions back to the one which you select. The keyboard shortcut **Ctrl+Z** also undoes just the last action.

Using The Properties Organiser

Every part of a form has a list of properties which can be changed. Some of these are accessible on the Formatting toolbar, but all of them are in the Properties organiser. In Design view, click on the **Properties** button:

This makes the Properties organiser appear. The properties shown relate to whatever section or control is selected in the form. We'll look at the properties for a text box.

The organiser has four pages plus a page which lists everything. Some of the pages need scrolling to reveal all their properties. First, the **Format** page.

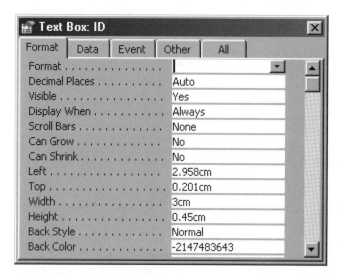

Look through these properties on a form to see where you could alter the font settings, the width and height of the box and its border.

The **Data** page deals with the data which comes from the table or query lying behind the form:

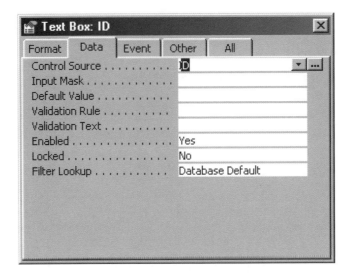

The most important property here is the **Control Source** which is the field to which the text box is bound.

The **Event** page can be ignored in this course. The **Other** page has one property of interest: **Tab Stop** which can be set to **No** so that tabbing through the form will not include this control. (Tabbing through will be mentioned more fully later.)

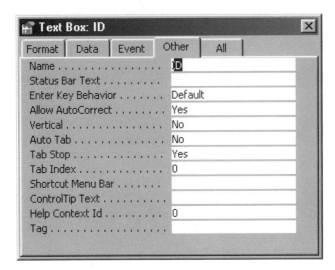

Creating A Form In Design View

Open the database.

Select **Forms** from the **Objects** list.

Select **New**.

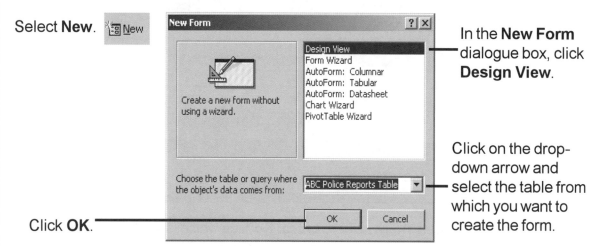

In the **New Form** dialogue box, click **Design View**.

Click on the drop-down arrow and select the table from which you want to create the form.

Click **OK**.

T
A
S
K

1. Ensure the **Police Records** database is open.

2. Create a form in Design view based on the **ABC Police Reports Table**.

Adding Or Removing A Form Header/Footer Or A Page Header/ Footer

Click **Form Header/ Footer** or **Page Header/ Footer** on the **View** menu.

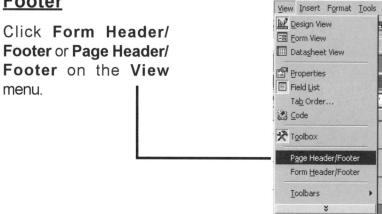

Page headers and footers appear at the top and bottom of each printed page. However, they don't appear in Form view.

Form headers and footers will appear at the top and bottom of a form in Form view and at the beginning and end of a printed form.

T
A
S
K

1. Select **Page Header/Footer** from the **View** menu.

2. Select **Form Header/Footer** from the **View** menu.

Creating A Bound Text Box

When creating a form in Design view, the **Field List** will be needed to link the form to the information in the database.

Should the list not be showing, select the **Field List** 🗏 icon from the toolbar.

The **Field List** should appear:

Select the fields needed from the field list to be positioned on the form.

To select:	Action to be carried out:
One field	Click the field.
A block of fields	Click the first field in the block, hold down the Shift key and click the last field in the block.
Non-adjacent fields	Hold down the Ctrl key and click the name of each field that you want to include.
All fields	Double-click the field list title bar.

Once selected, drag the field or fields from the field list and position them on the form or report in the details section.

Tip: It may be easier to move only a few fields at a time.

T A S K

1. Resize the form by following the instructions on page 53.

*2. Increase the size of the **Details** section by placing the cursor at the top of the **Page Footer** bar. A double-headed arrow will appear. Click and drag down to create extra space.*

*3. Drag all the fields into the **Detail** section and position as shown over the page.*

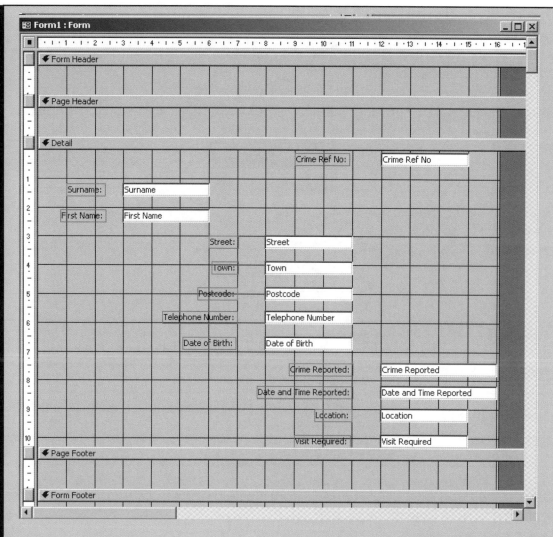

4. Adjust the label and text boxes so that the data is clearly displayed.

Continued in the next task …

Formatting Labels And Text Boxes

Labels and text boxes can be formatted, whilst in Design view, so that the data appears in bold, italic, underlined. Additionally, the alignment, colour, font size, font type and borderlines can all be adjusted to improve the way in which the form appears.

To change the formatting of the individual label and text control boxes:

Click to select the control box. Click the required formatting option from the Form Formatting toolbar.

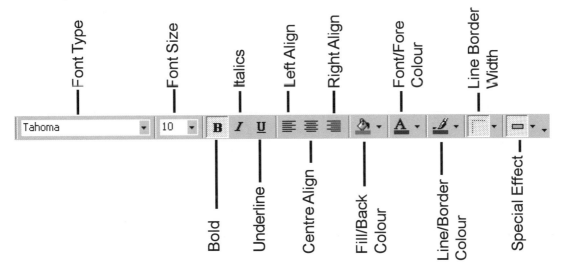

Alternatively, right-click on the control box and the options will be available from the list.

When changing the formatting for multiple control boxes, more than one can be selected at a time by holding down the **Shift** key when selecting the boxes.

To resize the control boxes to fit the text after changing the formatting, select **Size** on the **Format** menu and then click **To Fit**. This will save the need to adjust each individual box using the drag handles.

Another technique is to get one control right and then use the **Format Painter** to transfer its formatting to other controls.

To transfer formatting from control A to control B:
        Click on control A
        Click on Format Painter
        Click on control B.

To transfer formatting from control A to more than one other control:
        Click in control A
        Double click on Format Painter
        Click on each of the 'target' controls in turn
        Click again on Format Painter to switch it off.

The Format Painter will transfer the formatting which can be set from the Formatting toolbar, but not other formatting like height and width which can only be changed from the Properties organiser.

T A S K

1. In Design view, set all the field heading controls to bold, right aligned, font size 10, font type Arial and special effect - raised.

2. Set the field data boxes to italics, left aligned, font size 10, font type Arial and special effect - sunken.

3. Resize the control boxes to fit the data.

4. Reposition the control boxes as necessary.

5. In the **Form Header** section, create a new heading **Crime Victims Details** in capital letters. Format the heading to bold, font size 24, font type Arial, centre aligned and special effect - raised.

6. Save the form with the name **ABC Crime Victims Details Form**.

Your form should appear similar to the one below:

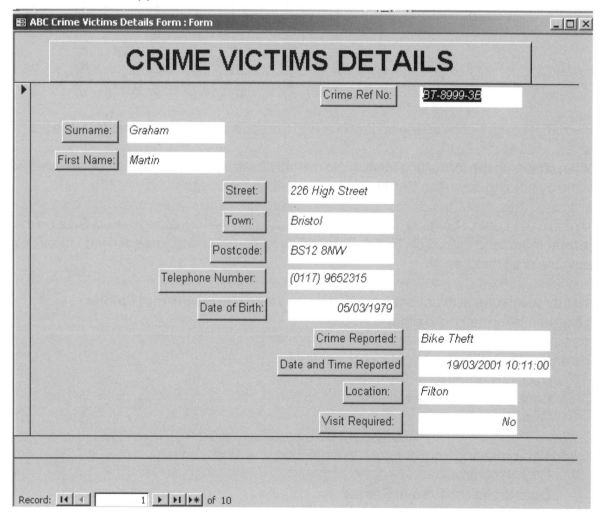

The Form And Section Selector

Having laid the form out, you may wish to alter the background settings of the form.

Microsoft Access allows you to format the entire form or an individual section.

To format the entire form, click the form selector.

To format an individual section, click the section selector.

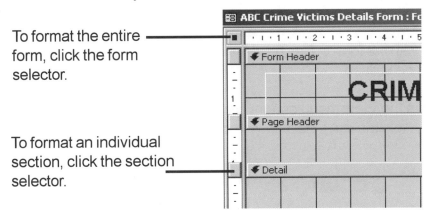

Click **AutoFormat** on the toolbar and select one of the formats in the list. (**NB** to prevent existing formatting from being lost, click **Options** and remove the tick from the font and colour check boxes.) To apply a background picture, the entire form must be selected.

TASK

1. Switch the **ABC Crime Victims Details Form** to Design view.

2. Format the entire form as **International** from the list of formats available. Do not change the font and colour of the control boxes.

3. Use **Save As** and name the altered form as **ABC International Crime Victims Details Form**. Close the form.

4. Re-open the **ABC Crime Victims Details Form** in Design view.

5. Select the **Detail** section only and change the fill colour to a light shade of blue.

6. Set the **Page Footer** and **Form Footer** sections only to the same shade.

7. Select the **Heading Label Box** in the form header section and set the font colour to White.

8. Select the **Form Header** section and change the fill colour to Black.

9. Switch to Form view to view the results.

10. Save the updated form with the name **ABC Crime Victims Details1 Form**.

Setting The Tab Order

When entering information into the form, the order in which the fields are set for data entry is known as the **Tab Order** - the order in which you can move through the form by pressing the **Tab** key or, usually by pressing **Enter** (**Return**). The tab order can be set to go from left to right and top to bottom or you can customise the order to meet your own requirements.

You must be working with the form in Design view, select **Edit** and **Select Form** to ensure that the tab order can be utilised.

Select **Tab Order** from the **View** menu or right click on the **Detail** section selector and select ⬛ Ta_b Order... from the list. The following dialogue box will appear:

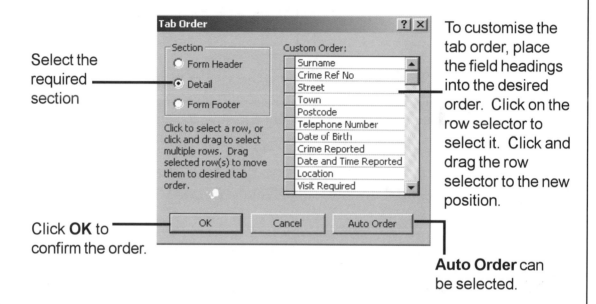

Select the required section

To customise the tab order, place the field headings into the desired order. Click on the row selector to select it. Click and drag the row selector to the new position.

Click **OK** to confirm the order.

Auto Order can be selected.

T A S K

1. *View the **ABC Crime Victims Details1 Form** in Design view.*

2. *Set the **Tab Order** so that the personal details are entered first, followed by the crime details, and the crime reference number is entered at the end.*

3. *Switch to Form view and press the **Tab** key to follow the order you have set. **Save** the changes to the form.*

Inserting Graphics

You can insert pictures (graphics or images) into a form. When you insert a picture, Microsoft Access stores the picture in your database file. An inserted object is always available. If you modify the picture on your form, the picture is changed in your database.

Open the form in Design view.

Click on the **Image** button ![image button] in the toolbox.

Click and drag on the form where you wish to insert the picture.

The **Insert Picture** dialogue box will open:

Click on the **Look in:** drop-down menu and select **3½ Floppy (A:)**.

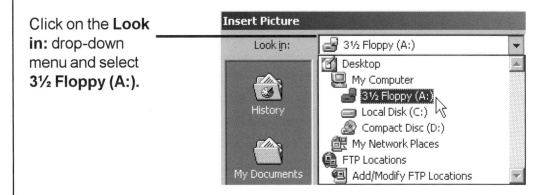

Select a picture and click **OK**.

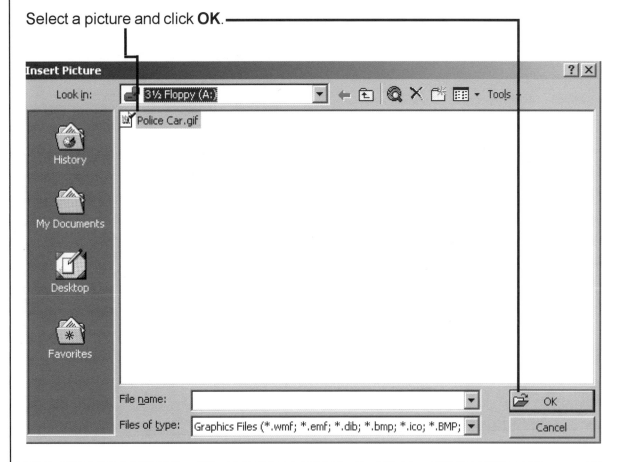

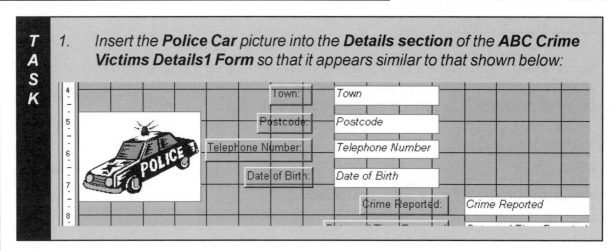

T A S K

1. *Insert the **Police Car** picture into the **Details section** of the **ABC Crime Victims Details1 Form** so that it appears similar to that shown below:*

Creating A Command Button

A command button can be used on a form to start an action or a set of actions. Actions which need to be carried out each time a form is used could be set as individual command buttons. You can create a command button on your own, or Microsoft Access can create your command button for you, using a wizard. The wizard speeds up the process of creating a command button because it does all the basic work for you. When you use a wizard, Access prompts you for information and then creates the command button based on your answers. You can create various types of command buttons by using the **Command Button Wizard**.

Open the form in Design view.

Make sure the **Control Wizards** button in the toolbox is on.

Click on the **Command Button** ▭ in the toolbox.

The mouse pointer will change to a cross with a box. Click where you want to position the command button.

This dialogue box will appear:

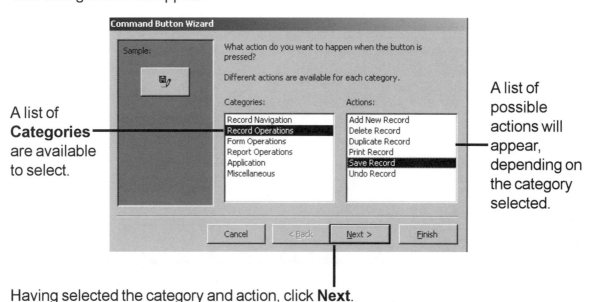

A list of **Categories** are available to select.

A list of possible actions will appear, depending on the category selected.

Having selected the category and action, click **Next**.

An example of the selection made will be shown here.

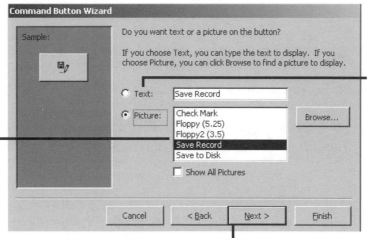

Select **Text** if text is to appear on the command button.

Select one of the pictures available to appear on the command button.

Once the desired option has been selected, click **Next**.

Add a name for the button should any modifications be necessary later.

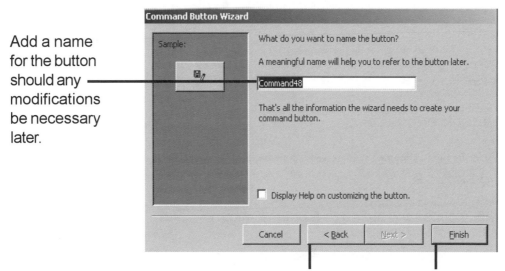

At this stage, to make any changes, click **Back** or click on **Finish**.

A command button has now been created and can be moved to an exact location in the design.

T A S K	1. Using the **ABC Crime Victims Details1 Form** in Design view.
	2. Create a command button to **Print Record**.
	3. Create a command button to **Save Record**.
	4. Create a command button to **Close** the form.
	5. Create a command button to **Add New record**.
	6. Place the command in suitable positions on the form.
	7. Switch to Form view and test the commands. Close the database. **(NB The Print Command will Print the Form each time it is clicked.)**

CONSOLIDATION EXERCISE

1. Open the **Television** database.

2. Create a new form using the **Design view**.

3. Include **Form Headers and Footers** and **Page Headers and Footers**.

4. Insert the heading **My Favourite Programmes** and format this as font type Tahoma, font size 28, bold and centre aligned. Resize to fit contents.

5. Select all the field data and label boxes and position these with the **Programme Name** at the top and all the other fields in a suitable layout below.

6. Make all the field labels bold, font size 12, font type Comic Sans and right aligned.

7. Make all the field data boxes italic, font size 12, font type Comic Sans and left aligned.

8. Set a suitable **Tab Order**.

9. Set the **AutoFormat** for the whole form as **Expedition**. Do not change the font and colour of the control boxes.

10. Create a command button to **Save** the record.

11. Create a command button to **Add New** record.

12. Create a command button to **Close** the form.

13. Save the form as **ABC Favourite Own Design Form**

14. Close the database.

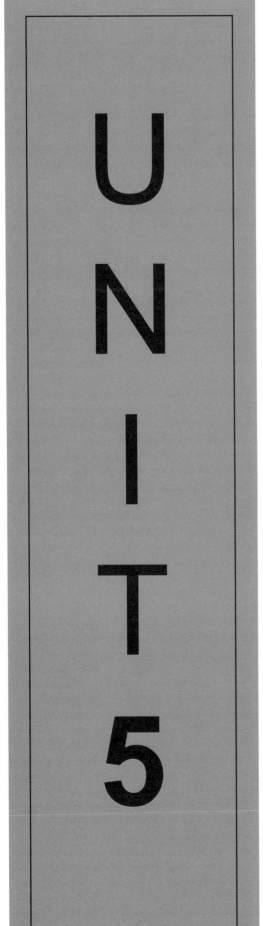

On completion of this unit, you will have learnt about and practised the following:

- **Copying The Table Structure**

  - Copying The Table Structure

- **Data Entry**

  - Entering Data Into The New Structure
  - Moving Fields

- **Finding And Replacing**

  - Finding Data
  - Finding And Replacing Data

- **Deleting Records**

  - Deleting Records
  - Editing Data In A Form

- **Copying Records From One Table To Another**

  - Copying Records From One Table To Another

- **Moving Records**

  - Moving Records

Copying The Table Structure

Copying The Table Structure

Copying a table structure allows the user to copy the design features and data from a table, creating an exact copy with a new name, within the same database file.

Open the database file.

Highlight the table of which you require the structure copy (do not open the table).

Click **Copy**

Click **Paste**

The **Structure Only** radio button just copies the design of the highlighted table. ⎯⎯⎯

The **Structure and Data** radio button copies the design and the data.

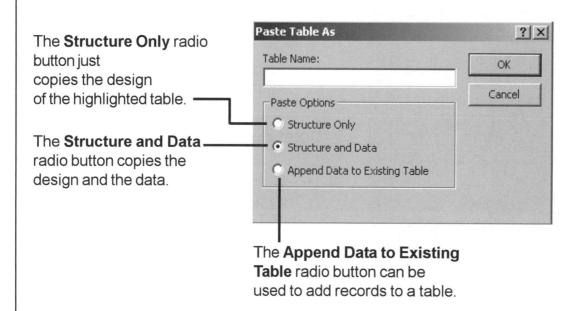

The **Append Data to Existing Table** radio button can be used to add records to a table.

Type in a new **Table Name**.

Click **OK** to confirm.

T A S K	1.	*Open the **Police Records** database.*
	2.	*Copy the **Structure Only** of the **Police Reports** table.*
	3.	*Name the table as **Police Reports Additional Data**.*

Data Entry

Entering Data Into The New Structure

Once the table structure has been copied, new data can be entered into the structure. A form can be created to input the data or the data can be inputted directly into the datasheet.

TASK

1. Enter the following data into the **ABC Police Reports Additional Data Table** in Datasheet view.

Record	Crime Ref No	Surname	First Name	Street	Town	Postcode	Telephone Number	Date of Birth	Crime Reported	Date and Time Reported	Location	Visit Required
1	LC-4556-5J	Packer	Steve	91 Baldwin Street	Bristol	BS15 7NW	(0117) 9765419	31/07/1978	Laptop Stolen from Car	30/11/2001 14:05:00	Kingswood	Yes
2	MP-7878-4M	Michaels	Dorothy	124 Parkfield Way	Bristol	BS15 9SE	(0117) 9745617	10/06/1986	Mobile Theft	25/09/2001 19:15:00	Mangotsfield	Yes
3	CS-5468-3C	Mooney	Kate	45 The Avenue	Bristol	BS19 2DT	(0117) 9845684	01/03/1980	Car Stolen	13/03/2001 05:00:00	Kingswood	No
4	HB-1499-2B	Hawkins	John	18 Holly Close	Bristol	BS16 5SW	(0117) 9586987	01/06/1951	House Burglary	22/01/2000 12:55:00	Kingswood	Yes
5	HW-1133-2G	Vines	Gemma	119 Maple Walk	Bristol	BS16 9DT	(0117) 9372605	26/04/1978	House Window Smashed	22/03/2000 12:12:00	Warmley	No
6	CC-4455-5C	Grant	John	2 Dennisworth	Bristol	BS16 9SW	(0117) 9345675	14/02/1965	Credit Cards Stolen	10/10/2000 11:05:00	Almondsbury	No
7	CT-1458-2C	Mitchell	Rose	12 King Street	Bristol	BS17 2SW	(0117) 9567296	12/05/1965	Car Stolen	22/01/2000 10:00:00	Downend	No
8	BT-8945-3B	Burton	Emma	121 Penny Street	Bristol	BS17 2SW	(0117) 9468133	12/12/1981	Bike Theft	20/07/2000 07:00:00	Stoke Gifford	No
9	CV-6589-3C	Smith	Paul	58 Abson Road	Swindon	SW5 5NW	(0119) 9586053	02/04/1973	Car Vandalised	10/05/2000 01:30:00	Wick	Yes
10	CS-5499-3C	Hendy	Mark	245 Whiteladies Road	Swindon	SW6 7NW	(0119) 9568452	05/07/1969	Car Stolen	16/03/2000 23:05:00	Dyrham	No

2. Close the table.

Moving Fields

It is possible to change the order of fields within a table to make data entry easier. Data should be entered in a logical sequence, for example **First Name**, **Surname** then **Address**; rather than **Surname**, **Address** then **First Name**.

To move a field in Datasheet View:

Click on the field heading to highlight the whole column.

Crime Reported	Date and Time Reported	Location	Visi
Laptop Stolen from Car	30/11/20 , 14:05:00	Kingswood	
Mobile Theft	25/09/2001 19:15:00	Mangotsfield	
Car Stolen	13/03/2001 05:00:00	Kingswood	
House Burglary	22/01/2000 12:55:00	Kingswood	
House Window Smashed	22/03/2000 12:12:00	Warmley	
Credit Cards Stolen	10/10/2000 11:05:00	Almondsbury	
Car Stolen	22/01/2000 10:00:00	Downend	
Bike Theft	20/07/2000 07:00:00	Stoke Gifford	
Car Vandalised	10/05/2000 01:30:00	Wick	
Car Stolen	16/03/2000 23:05:00	Dyrham	

Click and drag the column to its new location. The thick black line indicates where the column will be placed.

Note: This action only affects the order in which fields are seen in the Datasheet view - the Design view is not affected. You can also alter the order of fields in Design view (by highlighting and dragging it to a new position). That change also changes the order in Datasheet view.

T A S K

1. *In the **ABC Police Reports Additional Data Table**, Datasheet view, move the **Date and Time Reported** field so that it appears after the **Crime Ref No** field.*

2. *Save the changes to the table and close the table.*

3. *In the **ABC Police Reports Table**, Datasheet view, move the **Date and Time Reported** field so that it appears after the **Crime Ref No** field.*

4. *Save the changes to the table and close the table.*

Finding And Replacing

Finding Data

One of the benefits of using a computerised database rather than a manual database is the speed at which information can be found. You can search a large database and pinpoint an exact piece of information quickly and accurately.

To find data in a table:

Ensure that you are in Datasheet view.

Click on the **Find** 🔍 button on the toolbar, or use the **Edit** menu, **Find** option.

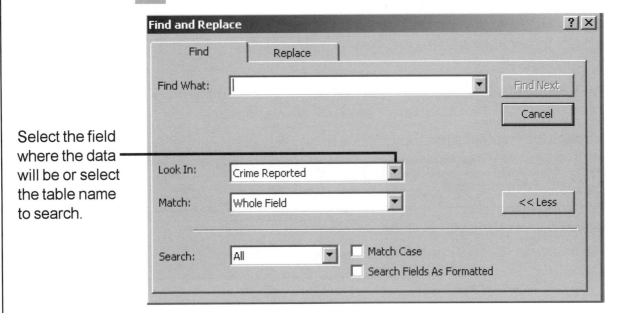

Select the field where the data will be or select the table name to search.

Type in the information you wish to find in the **Find What:** box.

Look in: - You can select to search just the current field, or the whole table.

Match: - You can search on the whole field, or on any part of the field, or just the first part of the field.

Search: - You can specify which direction to search in from the current record, ie forwards, backwards or both directions.

Match Case - When ticked, only data that follows the format typed in will be displayed

Find Next - Finds the next matching data.

Once the data you are looking for has been found, **Close** the **Find and Replace** dialogue box and the data will stay highlighted.

T A S K

1. In the **ABC Police Reports Table**, *Datasheet view, find* **Bath**.

2. Find the **Date of Birth 04/08/1967** for **Pauline Jones**. *The* **Date of Birth** *is incorrect.* **Delete** *the* **Date of Birth** *for* **Pauline Jones**.

Finding And Replacing Data

As well as being able to find data quickly using our database, we are able to find and replace data quickly. This is especially useful if changes need to be made to lots of records at once.

To find and replace data in a table:

Ensure that you are in Datasheet view.

Click on the **Find** 🔍 button on the toolbar, or use the **Edit** menu, **Find** option.

Click on the **Replace** tab.

Type in the data that you wish to find in the **Find What:** box ——

Type in the new data you wish to insert in the **Replace With:** box

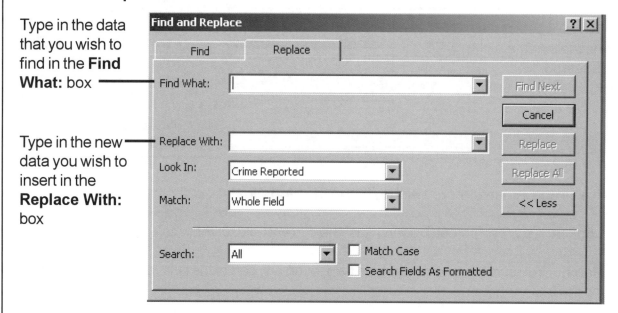

Find and Replace	? ✕
Find Replace	
Find What:	Find Next
	Cancel
Replace With:	Replace
Look In: Crime Reported	Replace All
Match: Whole Field	<< Less
Search: All ☐ Match Case ☐ Search Fields As Formatted	

Look in: - You can select to search just the current field, or the whole table.

Match: - You can search on the whole field, or on any part of the field, or just the first part of the field.

Search: - You can specify which direction to search in from the current record, ie forwards, backwards or both directions.

Match Case: When ticked: only data that follows the format typed in will be displayed.

Find Next: Finds the next matching data.

Click **Find Next.**

If you wish to replace the located field, click **Replace**. If you do not want to replace the field, click **Find Next** (until you locate one that you do want to replace).

Replace All allows the user to replace all data matching the **Find What** criteria in one go. It is best to place the cursor in the field to be searched and select the **Current Field** in **Look in:**. This will ensure that unwanted changes are not made.

Close the **Find and Replace** dialogue box when all changes have been made.

T A S K	1.	In the ***ABC Police Reports Table***, *Datasheet view, replace **Car** with **Vehicle**.*
	2.	*Close and save the **ABC Police Reports Table**.*
	3.	*In the **ABC Police Reports Additional Data Table**, Datasheet view, replace **Car** with **Vehicle**.*
	4.	*Close and save the **ABC Police Reports Additional Data Table**.*
	5.	*Close the **Police Reports** database.*

Deleting Records

Deleting Records

Take care when deleting records as, once deleted, the record is gone forever! If you delete a record by mistake, you will have to retype the whole record again as a new record.

To delete a record:

Ensure that you are in Datasheet view.

Click on the **Row Selector** for the record you wish to delete. The record will be highlighted.

Click on the **Delete Record** button on the toolbar.

The record now disappears from view, but it is not actually deleted until you confirm the deletion.

Click **Yes** to confirm deletion. ——————————

T	1.	In the **Television** database, open the **ABC Favourite Programmes**
A		**Table** in Datasheet view, delete the record for **Kilroy.**
S		
K	2.	Close the **Television** database.

Editing Data In A Form

Data can be modified on a *form* in much the same way as on a table. On columnar forms, you can only see one record at a time, so the **Find** facility is even more useful than it is on a table.

Copying Table To Table

Copying Records From One Table To Another Table

When using tables within a database, you may need to copy or move records from one table to another. It may be the case that having separate tables of information is not required and the information can be amalgamated into one table. It may also be that you need to export some of your data for someone else to use.

To copy records:

Open the table containing the data to be copied in Datasheet view.

Highlight the required records or, if required, select all the records by clicking **Edit** and clicking **Select All Records**.

Click **Edit**.

Click **Copy** (or use the shortcut **Ctrl+C**).

Minimise the table.

Open the table where the records are to be copied in to.

Click **Edit**. ——————

Click **Paste Append**. ——————

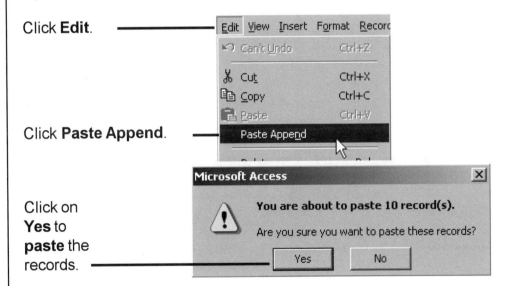

Click on **Yes** to **paste** the records. ——————

Moving Records

Moving Records

Open the table containing the data to be moved.

Highlight the required records or, if required, select all the records by clicking **Edit** and clicking **Select All Records**.

Click **Edit**.

Click **Cut** (or use the shortcut **Ctrl+X**).

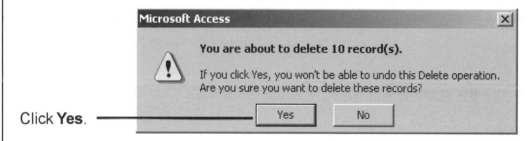

Click **Yes**.

Minimise the table.

Open the table where the records are to be moved to.

Click **Edit**.

Click **Paste Append**.

Click **Yes** to **Paste** the records into the table.

**T
A
S
K**

1. Open the **Police Records** database.

2. Open the **ABC Police Reports Additional Data Table**.

3. Move all the records from the **ABC Police Reports Additional Data Table** to the **ABC Police Reports Table**.

4. Save and close both tables and the **Police Records** database.

5. Compact the databases on your floppy disk.

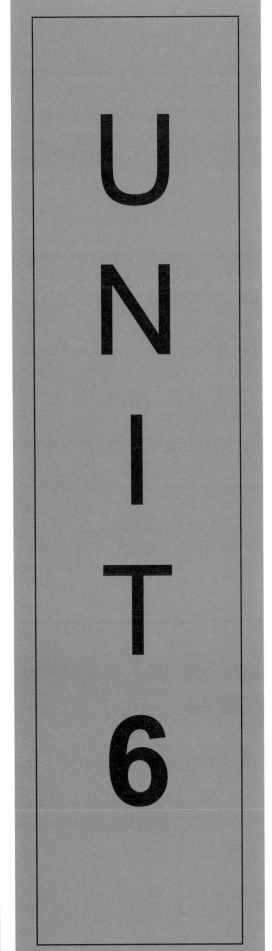

On completion of this unit, you will have learnt about and practised the following:

- **Queries**

  - What Is A Query?
  - What Types Of Query Are There?
  - Creating A New Select Query
  - Entering Field Names

- **Criteria**

  - Selection Criteria
  - Wildcards
  - Entering SelectionCriteria
  - Sorting A Query
  - Query Result
  - Saving A Query
  - Running Multiple Search Criteria
  - Sorting Within Sort
  - Criteria On Date Fields

- **Action Queries**

  - About Action Queries
  - Creating A Make-Table Query
  - Creating An Update Query
  - Creating An Append Query
  - Creating A Delete Query

Queries

What Is A Query?

A query is simply an Access object which implements a question you ask of the database, eg who lives in a particular town, which employees started before a certain date etc. The resulting information from querying the database can be sorted and specified fields can be shown. Queries can be saved.

What Types Of Query Are There?

An enormous number of queries are available. There are many different variations of queries that can be created, however there are only two main types of query: **Select** and **Action** queries.

Select

Select queries are those in which the data resulting from the query is viewed on screen and made available to appear in forms, reports or further queries. The select query is the most common.

Action

Action queries are different from select queries in that they perform an operation. The four most straightforward different types of action queries are:

- Make-Table
- Update
- Append
- Delete

Creating A New Select Query

Click **Queries** from the **Objects** menu and double-click on **Create Query in Design view.**

The **Show Table** dialogue box will appear:

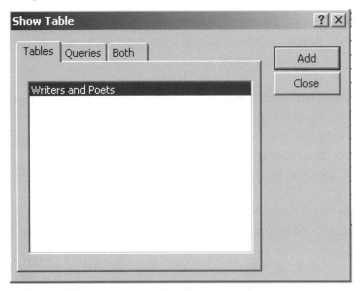

Click on the table you wish to use and click **Add**, then **Close**.

The field names from your table appear here.

The field names are entered here.

The search criteria are entered here.

The sort order can be set here.

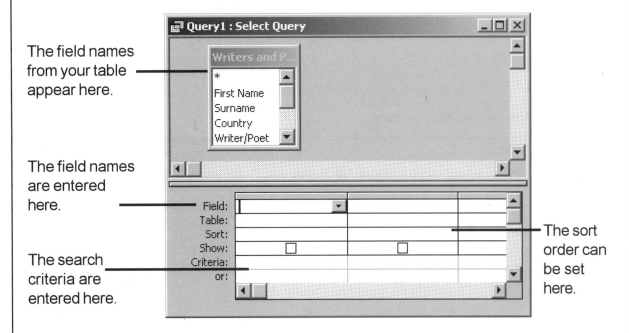

The fields to be used for the query can now be chosen, the sort order specified and the criteria entered.

T A S K	1.	*Open the **Personal Interests** database.*
	2.	*Create a **Select Query** based on the **Writers and Poets** table.*
		***Do not** specify any criteria until the next task.*

Entering Field Names

You need to tell Access which fields to include in the query. You can do this either individually or include all the field names from a table at the same time. Only the fields that you select here will appear in the resulting query.

To enter field names individually:

Click on the field name of the required field
and drag down into the first field box available
or
Double-click on the field name required
and it will automatically be placed in the
first available field box.

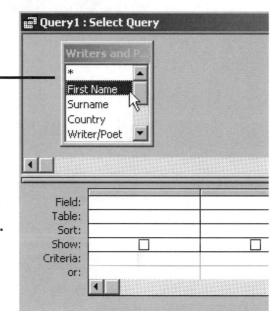

**NB You do not have to select all fields and
the order of the fields can be changed.**

To enter all the fields from a table:

Double-click on the table name to select all fields.

Click on the highlighted
list and drag down to the
Field row in the grid.

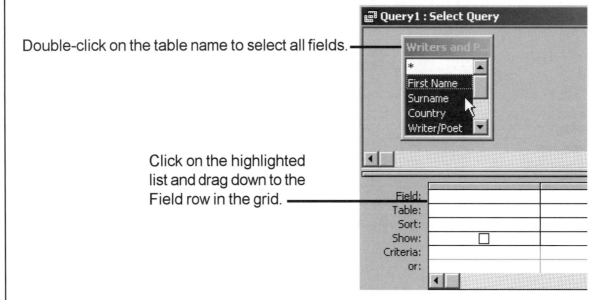

**NB You can also enter fields by dragging or double-clicking the asterisk. This,
however, inserts the fields in the query as if they were a single field, so
you can't get at an individual field to apply criteria or sorting to it.**

**T
A
S
K**

1. *In your new **Select Query**, enter all the fields from the **Writers and Poets**
table.*

Criteria

Criteria are restrictions you place on a query to identify the specific records you want to work with.

Selection Criteria

There are a number of selection criteria that can be used to identify the records.

Expression	Meaning
<	Less than
<=	Less than or equal to
>	More than
>=	More than or equal to
=	Equal to
Between...And	Select a range
Is Null	Blank fields displayed
Is Not Null	Fields with data displayed
<>	Not equal to

Or	eg "Pass" **Or** "Refer", the OR operator will find both **passes** and **refers.**
And	eg "1/1/1989" And "1/1/1990", the AND operator will display both dates.
Not	eg Not "Refer", the NOT operator will find anything other than Refer.
Yes	In a logical field to find the positive results type in **Yes**.
No	In a logical field to find the negative results type in **No**.

Wildcards

You use wildcard characters when you are specifying a value that you want to find:

- where you know only part of the value
- which contains a specific character or matches a certain pattern

You can use the following characters in the **Find** and **Replace** dialogue boxes, or in **Queries** and **Expressions**, to find such things as field values and records (must be entered into the **Criteria** box).

Character	Usage	Example
*	Matches any number of characters. It can be used as the first, last or both in the character string.	wh* finds **what**, **white** and **why**. *ght finds **light**, **right** and **bright**
?	Matches any single alphabetic character.	B?ll finds **ball**, **bell** and **bill**
[ ]	Matches any single character within the brackets.	B[ae]ll finds **ball** and **bell** but not bill
!	Matches any character not in the brackets.	B[!ae]ll finds **bill** and **bull** but not ball and bell
-	Matches any one of a range of characters. You must specify the range in ascending order (A to Z, not Z to A)	B[a-c]d finds **bad**, **bbd**, and **bcd**
#	Matches any single numeric character.	1#3 finds **103**, **113**, **123**

Entering Selection Criteria

You will need to be in Query Design view to be able to enter selection criteria.

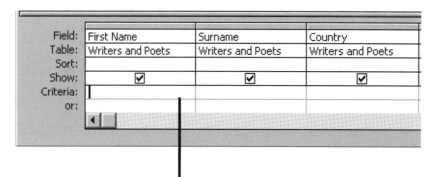

Enter criteria in the appropriate **Criteria** box.

Sorting A Query

Click in the **Sort** row of the appropriate field.
Click on the down arrow.
Select **Ascending** or **Descending** as appropriate from the drop-down list.

Click on the arrow in the sort row of the appropriate field and select ascending or descending.

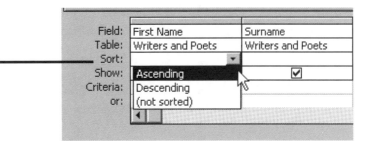

NB   Applying a sort in a query enables you to save the sort with the query. Therefore, every time the query is run, the data will be automatically sorted for you. Suppose new data has been entered on the table since you last ran the query. Running the query again will apply the sort afresh.

> **T**
> **A**
> **S**
> **K**
>
> 1.   *Enter the necessary criteria needed to obtain only the records where the writer/poet is described as a **Poet**.*
>
> 2.   *Sort ascending the query according to the writer's surname.*

Query Result

When all the fields and selection criteria have been entered into the **Query Design**, switch to Datasheet view to display the results.

Switching between the Design and Datasheet ![icon] views will allow you to modify the query to ensure you achieve the correct results.

Saving A Query

Click **Save**. ![save icon]

Type in a relevant **Query Name**.

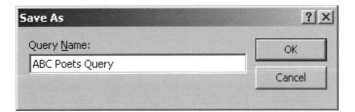

Click **OK**.

> **T**
> **A**
> **S**
> **K**
>
> 1.   *Check the result of the query (you should have 6 records).*
>
> 2.   *Save the query with the name **ABC Poets Query**.*

T A S K	*Using the **Writers and Poets** table, run each of the following select queries and save with the name provided:*
	1. *Find all the writers/poets whose country is **England**, show only the fields **First Name**, **Surname**, **Country** and **Writer/Poet**. Set an **Ascending Sort** according to **Surname**. Save as **ABC England Query.***
	2. *Find all the **Female** writers/poets, show only the fields **First Name Surname**, **Country**, **Gender** and **Item of Work**. Save as **ABC Female Writers Query**.*
	3. *Find all the writers/poets that were born between **1750** and **1850**, show **all** the fields. Set an **Ascending Sort** on **Year Born**. Save as **ABC 1750 to 1850 Query**.*
	4. *Find all the writers/poets whose surname begins with the letter **S**, show **all** the fields. Set a **Descending Sort** on **First Name**. Save as **ABC Surname S Query**.*

Running Multiple Search Criteria

The queries just produced have only found records based on one criterion per search. However, it may be necessary to define your search even further to find English poets.

This would be displayed as below:

Field:	First Name	Surname	Country	Writer/Poet	Year Born
Table:	Writers and Poets	Writers and Poets	Writers and Poets	Writers and Poets	Writers and Poets
Sort:					
Show:	☑	☑	☑	☑	☑
Criteria:			"England"	Like "*Poet*"	
or:					

The query is set up in exactly the same way as a normal select query. The only difference is that you now have a second search going on in the other field.

You may also need to find different items within the same field, such as finding writers from Scotland and England.

This would be displayed as:

Field:	First Name	Surname	Country	
Table:	Writers and Poets	Writers and Poets	Writers and Poets	\
Sort:				
Show:	☑	☑	☑	
Criteria:			"Scotland" Or "England"	
or:				

Works with the addition of the word **Or**

**T
A
S
K**

*Using the **Writers and Poets** table, run each of the following **Multiple Search** queries and save with the name provided:*

1. Find all the **Poets** from **Scotland**, show only the fields **First Name**, **Surname**, **Country** and **Writer/Poet**. Save as **ABC Scottish Poets Query**.

2. Find all the **Male** writers/poets born in the **1700**s, show only the fields **First Name**, **Surname**, **Country Writer/Poet**, **Year Born** and **Year Died**. Sort in **Descending** order on the **Year Born** field. Save as **ABC Males born 1700 Query**.

3. Find all the writers/poets born in the **1700**s from **Scotland** or **Ireland**, show **all** the fields. Sort in **Ascending** order on the **Surname** Field. Save as **ABC Born 1700 in Scotland or Ireland Query**.

Sorting Within Sort

The multiple sort is an easy way of creating a list of sorted details to make finding data easier.

For example, sorting **First Name** within **Surname** could be created by running a select query and sorting both fields, as below:

Field:	Surname	First Name
Table:	Writers and Poets	Writers and Poets
Sort:	Ascending	Ascending
Show:	☑	☑
Criteria:		
or:		

The effect of this sort will sort the Surnames in ascending order and within each sorted surname it will sort ascending the First names. The fields must be placed in the correct order to do this, with the most important sort first. An example of this multiple sort is shown below:

The Surnames are in alphabetical order.

Surname	First Name
Austen	Jane
Bronte	Charlotte
Bronte	Emily
Browning	Robert
Burns	Robert
Chaucer	Geoffrey
Chekov	Anton
Dickens	Charles
Dostoevsky	Fyodor
Dumas	Alexandre
Faulkner	William
Goethe	Johann Wolfgang von
Joyce	James
Keats	John
Melville	Herman
Milton	John
Scott	Walter
Shakespeare	William
Swift	Jonathan
Verne	Jules

Notice that the First Names are also sorted within the Surname groups.

TASK

1. Create a new query on the **Writers and Poets** table.

2. Sort **First Name** within **Surname** and show **all** the fields.

3. Save the query as **ABC First Name in Surname Sorted Query**.

4. Close the query and the database.

Criteria On Date Fields

A little care is needed in applying query criteria to date fields. When you see a date in a field, Access has actually stored a code number which it formats to look like a date. This means that, when dates are entered into criteria, they must be carefully labelled as dates. The convention for doing this is to place a hash [#] either side of the date. Usually you will find that Access will do this for you, but it's best to check.

T A S K

1. *Open **Personal Details.mdb**. You are to create some queries on **Birthdays Table**. All the queries should list Forename, Surname and Birthday.*

2. *Create a query showing birthdays after 7th May 2002. You should find that you can type in a variety of date formats. All the acceptable entries will be accepted within Access as*
    >#17/05/02#

    Sometimes, Access will think you're trying to type in a time reference and will interpret what you write as
    >#17:05:02#

    In this case, you would need to retype.
    *Save the query as **ABC After May 17 Query**.*

3. *Modify the previous query to make it include May 17th. Save as an update of the original query.*

4. *Create a query to show birthdays between 17th May 2002 and 6th Sept 2002 inclusive. You can experiment with two ways of writing the criterion:*
    >=#17/05/02# And <=#06/09/02#

    Between #17/05/02# And #06/09/02#

    These two will give the same result. If you wanted to include May 17th but not Sept 6th, you could adapt the first approach to:
    >=#17/05/02# And <#06/09/02#

    *Save the query as **ABC Between Dates Query**.*

5. *Close any open queries and close the database.*

Action Queries

About Action Queries

You can create **action queries** in the same way as **select queries**. Action queries are used to make bulk changes to the data rather than simply searching and displaying the resulting data.

Type of Query	Function
Make-table query	Creates a new table resulting from the criteria specified.
Update query	Changes/updates the specified data.
Append query	Adds records from one table to another table.
Delete query	Deletes records from a table.

The best and safest way to run an **action** query is to first create a standard **select** query, to ensure that the query is selecting correct records. It could be that the criteria you have specified is not right and it could be easy to delete or change the wrong set of data.

Once **action** queries have been run, the changes cannot be reversed.

Creating A Make-Table Query

Create a select query specifying the criteria you require to be viewed in your new table.

Check that the resulting query has found the correct data. If it hasn't, you will need to amend your criteria.

Only once the resulting query is correct should you move on.

Switch to the **Design view**.

Click **Query** on the menu bar.

Click **Make-Table Query**.

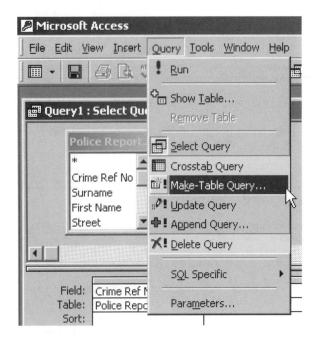

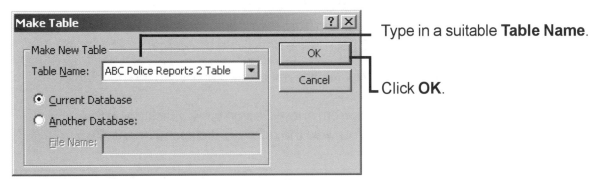

Type in a suitable **Table Name**.

Click **OK**.

Close the **Make-Table** query.

The save changes to the query dialogue box will appear:

Click **Yes**.

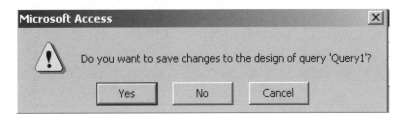

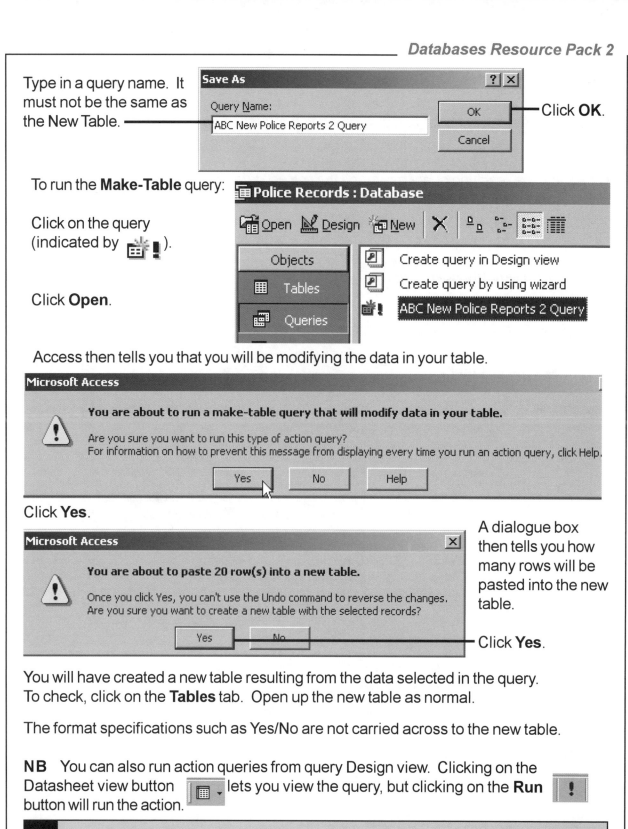

Type in a query name. It must not be the same as the New Table. ——

Save As   ? ✕

Query Name:

ABC New Police Reports 2 Query

OK —— Click **OK**.

Cancel

To run the **Make-Table** query:

Click on the query (indicated by ▦▌).

Click **Open**.

Police Records : Database

📭 Open ☒ Design 📭 New   ✕   ᵈ□   ⁝⁝   ⁞⁞⁞⁞   ▦

Objects

▦ Tables

▦ Queries

📭 Create query in Design view

📭 Create query by using wizard

▦▌ ABC New Police Reports 2 Query

Access then tells you that you will be modifying the data in your table.

Microsoft Access

⚠ **You are about to run a make-table query that will modify data in your table.**

Are you sure you want to run this type of action query?
For information on how to prevent this message from displaying every time you run an action query, click Help.

Yes   No   Help

Click **Yes**.

Microsoft Access   ✕

⚠ **You are about to paste 20 row(s) into a new table.**

Once you click Yes, you can't use the Undo command to reverse the changes.
Are you sure you want to create a new table with the selected records?

Yes   No

A dialogue box then tells you how many rows will be pasted into the new table.

—— Click **Yes**.

You will have created a new table resulting from the data selected in the query. To check, click on the **Tables** tab. Open up the new table as normal.

The format specifications such as Yes/No are not carried across to the new table.

NB You can also run action queries from query Design view. Clicking on the Datasheet view button ▦ ▾ lets you view the query, but clicking on the **Run** ▌ button will run the action.

T
A   1.   *Open the **Police Records** database.*
S
K   2.   *Use **make-table** query to create a new table consisting of all the records in the **ABC Police Reports Table**. Call the new table **ABC Police Reports 2 Table**. Call the query **ABC New Police Reports 2 Query**.*

3.   *Open the **ABC Police Reports 2 Table** to view the contents.*

4.   *Adjust the fields so that the contents can be viewed. Check the design of the table and check the data is correct and amend if necessary. Close and save the changes*

T A S K	1.	Create a new table using the **ABC Police Records 2 Table** that shows all the people who live in **Bath**. Show all the fields. Call the new table **ABC Bath Table**. Call the query **ABC Town Bath Query** (there should be 2 records).
	2.	Print out the records from the new table.
	3.	Close the table.

Creating An Update Query

Create a select query, specifying the criteria that you wish to be updated.

Check that the resulting query has found the correct data. Some alterations to the criteria selection may be required.

Only once the resulting query is correct should you move on.

Switch to the **Design view**.

Click **Query** on the menu bar.

Click **Update Query**. ─────────

An **Update To** row has now appeared.

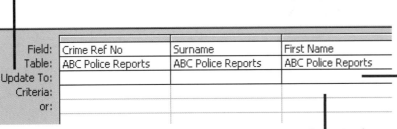

Type in the word or words in the relevant field. On running the query, it will change the old words with the new ones.

Type in the word(s) to be replaced in the relevant field.

Click **Save**.

Type in a suitable name and click **OK**.

Close the query.

To run the **update query**:

Click on the query (indicated by ::⏘!).

Click **Open**.
Click **Yes**.
Click **Yes**.

To view the changes, click on the **Tables** tab. Open the table as normal.

> **T A S K**
>
> 1.   Create an **update query** on the **ABC Police Reports 2 Table** to change all instances of **Vehicle Stolen** to **Vehicle Theft.**
>
> 2.   Save the **update query** with the name **ABC Vehicle Theft Query**.
>
> 3.   Close the query.

Creating An Append Query

Create a select query on the table that you wish to copy the data from.

Select all fields ————————

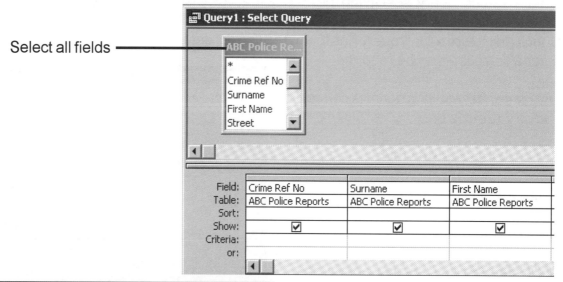

Click **Query**.

Click **Append Query**.

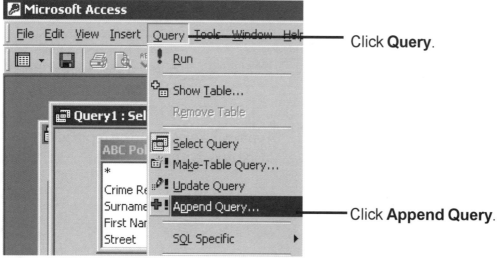

Select the table that you wish the copied data to be pasted into from the drop-down list.

Click **OK**.

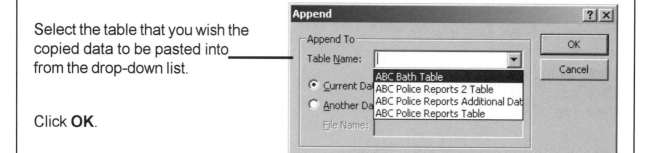

Click **Save**.

Type in a suitable query name that differs from the table names.

Click **OK**.

Close the query.

To run the **append query**:

Click on the query (indicated by).

Click **Open**.
Click **Yes**.
Click **Yes**.

To view changes, click on the **Tables** tab. Open the table as normal.

NB The paste append will not work with records that are duplicated within both tables if a primary key has been set. By clicking **Yes,** it will continue to paste all other records without any problems. Alternatively, the primary key can be removed before appending.

T A S K	1.	Create an append query to copy the records of people living in **Swindon** from the **ABC Police Records 2 Table** to the **ABC Bath Table**. Save the query as **ABC Appending Swindon Query**.
	2.	Open the **ABC Bath Table** and print out the records.
	3.	Close the table.

Creating A Delete Query

Create a select query, specifying the criteria that you wish to be deleted.

Check the resulting query has found the correct data.

Switch to the Design view.

Click on **Query** on the toolbar.

Click on **Delete Query**.

Click on **Save**.

Save the query with a suitable name.
Click **OK**.
Close the query.
To run the **delete query**.

Click on the query (indicated by).

Click **Open**.
Click **Yes**.
Click **Yes**.

To view the changes, click on the **Tables** tab. Open the table as normal.

T	1.	*Ensure you are working on the **Police Records** database.*
A		
S	2.	*Create a delete query to delete the records for all the people living in*
K		***Swindon** and **Bath** from the **ABC Police Reports 2 Table**. Save the*
		*query as **ABC Delete Swindon and Bath Query**.*
	3.	*Close the database.*
	4.	*Compact the **Police Records** database.*

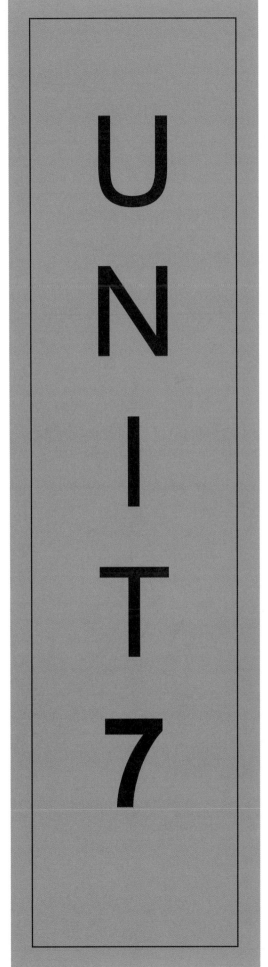

On completion of this unit, you will have learnt about and practised the following:

- **Indexes**

  - Using Indexes
  - Troubleshooting Problems With Sorting And Indexes
  - Single Field Index
  - Multiple Field indexes

- **Filters**

  - About Filter
  - Using A Filter
  - Using A Filter Excluding Selection
  - Using Filter By Form

Indexes

Using Indexes

An index helps Access find and sort records faster. Access uses indexes in a table as you would use an index in a book: to find data, it looks up the location of the data in the index. You can create indexes based on a single field or on multiple fields. Table indexes are usually relatively easy to add, modify and remove. The main tasks involved in adding indexes are analysing requirements and deciding which indexes are and are not necessary to provide the desired performance. Too many indexes placed where not necessary will slow down the database dramatically. A primary key field is automatically indexed.

Troubleshooting Problems With Sorting And Indexes

If your index does not work, you may have sorted the field using the automatic **A/Z** buttons. This overrides any index, so you need to go to Datasheet view, click **Remove Filter/Sort** on the **Records** menu. This will remove any sorts from your table and you can then go on and create your index in Design view.

Single Field Index

The **Single Field Index** is applied in the field properties section of the Table Design view. Click the row selector against the field that you wish to apply the **Single Index**.

Click on the drop-down arrow
of the **Indexed** properties box.

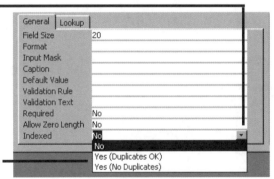

A selection of
Yes (Duplicates OK)
Yes (No Duplicates)

Yes (Duplicates OK) will sort and will allow duplicate data entry.
Yes (No Duplicates) will sort but will not allow duplicate data entries.

T A S K	
1.	Open the **ABC Police Reports Table** in the **Police Records** database. Remove the primary key from the **Crime Ref No** field.
2.	Ensure that the single field index is set to **No** for the **Crime Ref No** field. Save the changes. View the changes in datasheet view.
3.	Click on the **Surname** field header, Click **A-Z** button.
4.	Remove any existing indexes. Apply a single field index (not allowing any duplicates) on the **Crime Ref No** field. View the datasheet. Save the changes.

Multiple Field Indexes

By specifying one index before another, the computer searches for the record using the first index but, should it encounter any duplicates, it will then switch to the second index and search using that one.

Any primary keys that had previously been inserted must be removed to enable the new index to be run.

If the table has an index already, but you wish to insert a new index, the original must be deleted to enable the new index to be applied.

Open the table in Design view.

Click on the **Indexes** button.

The **Indexes** dialogue box will appear:

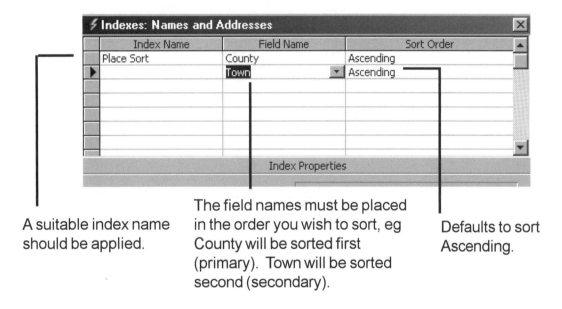

A suitable index name should be applied.

The field names must be placed in the order you wish to sort, eg County will be sorted first (primary). Town will be sorted second (secondary).

Defaults to sort Ascending.

The index set above needs only one name. If another index name is applied, it will assume that it is a completely separate index. To view the index applied, you will need to close the table and reopen.

T A S K

1. Using the **ABC Police Reports Table**, remove any existing indexes.

2. Using the index name **Name**, apply a **multiple index** on the name fields with the **Surname** as the **primary** field and **First Name** as the **secondary** field.

3. Save and print the datasheet view after applying the index.

4. Close the table and the database.

Filters

About Filters

The main advantage of using filters is that they can be applied directly to objects such as tables without the need to design and build a query from scratch. This provides the user with the control, but without encumbering the database with lots of queries.

Using A Filter

Ensure you have a table open.

Click in the item that you wish to find.

Writers and Poets : Table

First Name	Surname	Country	Writer/Poet	
Jane	Austen	England	Novelist	17
▶ Robert	Browning	England	Poet|	18
Robert	Burns	Scotland	Poet	17
Geoffrey	Chaucer	England	Poet	13

Click on the **Filter By Selection** button on the toolbar.

The **Filter** command will have filtered out all other data, just leaving your selection displayed, as below:

Writers and Poets : Table

First Name	Surname	Country	Writer/Poet	Year Born
▶ Robert	Browning	England	Poet	1812
Robert	Burns	Scotland	Poet	1759
Geoffrey	Chaucer	England	Poet	1340?
Johann Wolfgang von	Goethe	Germany	Poet	1749
John	Keats	England	Poet	1795
John	Milton	England	Poet	1608
✳				

To remove the filter, click on the **Remove Filter** button.

When closing the table, it will ask you if you want to save the changes. Click **No.**

T A S K	1.	Open the **Personal Interests** database.
	2.	Open the **Writers and Poets** table.
	3.	Apply a filter to find all the **Novelists**.
	4.	Print out the records.
	5.	Remove the filter.

Using A Filter Excluding Selection

You can also filter for records that do not have certain data.

After selecting the data, right-click it, and then click **Filter Excluding Selection**.

Country	Writer/Poet	Year Born	Year
England	Novelist	1775	
England	Poet		
Scotland	Poet		
England	Poet		
Russia	Stories/P		
England	Novelist		
Russia	Novelist		
France	Novelist/[		
America	Novelist		
Germany	Poet		
Ireland	Author		
America	Novelist		
England	Poet		

(Context menu: Filter By Selection / **Filter Excluding Selection** / Filter For: / Remove Filter/Sort / Sort Ascending / Sort Descending / Cut / Copy / Paste / Insert Object...)

The filter command will have filtered out the selection, leaving all other records.

First Name	Surname	Country	Writer/Poet	Year Born
Robert	Browning	England	Poet	1
Robert	Burns	Scotland	Poet	1
Geoffrey	Chaucer	England	Poet	1
Anton	Chekov	Russia	Stories/Plays	1
Alexandre	Dumas	France	Novelist/Dramatist	1
Johann Wolfgang von	Goethe	Germany	Poet	1
James	Joyce	Ireland	Author	1
John	Keats	England	Poet	1
John	Milton	England	Poet	1
Walter	Scott	Scotland	Novelist/Poet	1
William	Shakespeare	England	Dramatist/Poet	1
Jonathan	Swift	Ireland	Author	1

<table>
<tr><td rowspan="5">**T A S K**</td><td>1.</td><td>*Open the table **Writers and Poets.***</td></tr>
<tr><td>2.</td><td>*Apply a **Filter Excluding Selection** to exclude all the **Poets**.*</td></tr>
<tr><td>3.</td><td>*Print out the records.*</td></tr>
<tr><td>4.</td><td>*Remove the filter.*</td></tr>
<tr><td>5.</td><td>*Close the table and the database.*</td></tr>
</table>

Using Filter By Form

If you want to choose the data you're searching for from a list without scrolling through all the records in a datasheet, or if you want to specify multiple criteria at once, use Filter By Form.

Click **Filter By Form** ⊞ on the toolbar to switch to the **Filter By Form** window. Criteria can be specified for the filter.

Click the field in which you want to specify the criteria to find the records that are required in the filtered list.

The criteria can be entered by selecting the value to be searched for from the drop-down list or by typing the data into the field. The criteria can consist of an expression.

If you specify criteria in more than one field, the filter displays records only if they contain the same data you specified in each of those fields.

Enter the criteria in this row. ⟶

The drop-down lists can be used to select criteria.

When the criteria has been specified, click **Apply Filter** ▽ on the toolbar.

	First Name	Surname	Country	Writer/Poet	Year Born
▶	William	Faulkner	America	Novelist	189
	Herman	Melville	America	Novelist	181
*					

To specify alternative criteria that records can have to be included in the filter's results, click the **Or** tab for the datasheet and enter more criteria.

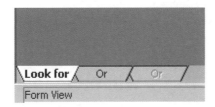

When the table is saved, Microsoft Access saves the filters you have created. You can then re-apply the filters when you need them.

T A S K

1. Open the database **Police Records**.

2. Open the **ABC Police Reports Table.**

3. Apply a **Filter By Form** to provide a list of people who were victim to any kind of crime involving a **Vehicle**.

f Birth	Crime Reported	
	Vehicle	▾

4. Apply the filter and print the results. Do not save the changes.

5. Undertake another **Filter By Form**, selecting all those who were victim to a **Vehicle** crime, which occurred **after 01/05/01**, and who live in **Bristol**.

Date and Time Reported		Town	
>=#01/05/2001#	▾	"Bristol" ▾	

6. Apply the filter and print the results. Do not save any changes.

C O N S O L I D A T I O N

1. Ensure you are using the table **Police Reports**.

2. Apply a **Filter By Form** to provide a list of people who were victim to any kind of house crime **before 01/01/02**.

3. Apply the filter and print the results.

4. Close the table and the database.

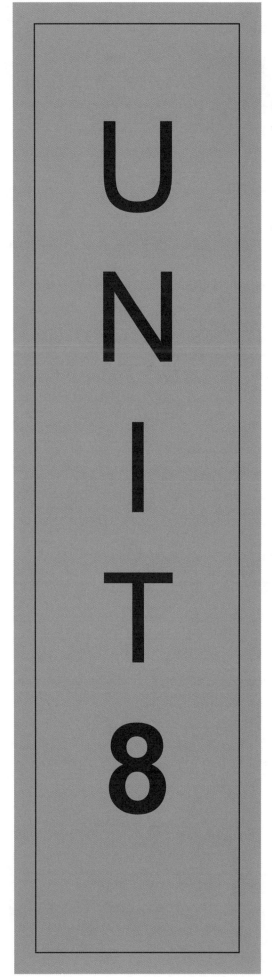

On completion of this unit, you will have learnt about and practised the following:

- **Reports**

  - About Reports
  - Creating An AutoReport
  - Creating A Report Using Report Wizard
  - Printing A Report
  - Modifying Reports
  - Totalling The Report
  - Ensuring Sorting And Grouping Are In Place

Reports

About Reports

Reports are used to display requested data in a visually pleasing format, designed to be printed. The design of the reports can be adjusted in the same way as forms.

Creating An AutoReport

Under **Objects**, select **Reports**.

Click **New**.

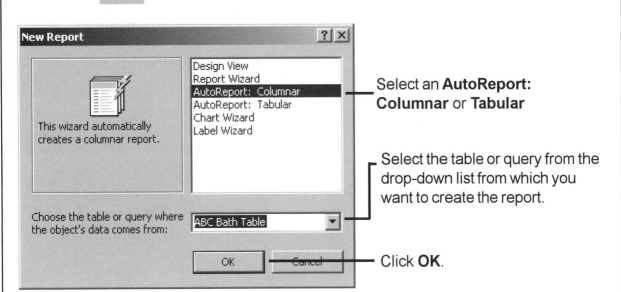

Select an **AutoReport: Columnar** or **Tabular**

Select the table or query from the drop-down list from which you want to create the report.

Click **OK**.

The finished report will appear on-screen.

Click **Save** and type in a suitable name.

T A S K

1. Open the **Police Records** database.

2. Create an **AutoReport** of your choice for the **ABC Bath Table**.

3. Save the report with the name **ABC Bath 1 Report**.

4. Close the database.

Creating A Report Using Report Wizard

Under **Objects**, select **Reports**.

Click **New**.

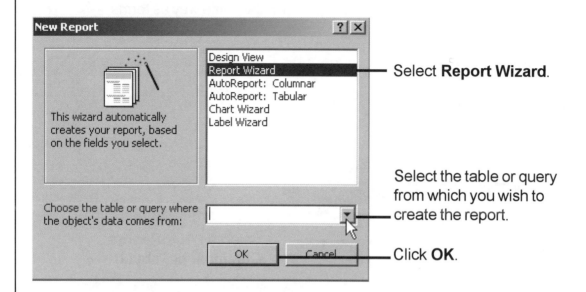

Select **Report Wizard**.

Select the table or query from which you wish to create the report.

Click **OK**.

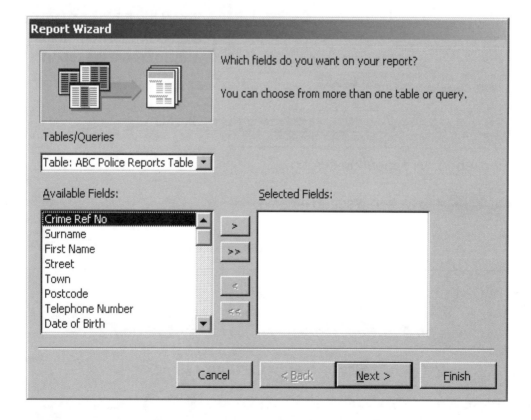

Select the fields that you will want to see in your report by clicking on the ▶ for individual fields or the ▶▶ for all fields.

Click **Next**.

T
A   1.   Open the **Police Records** database.
S
K   2.   Using the **ABC Police Reports Table**, create a report using the **Report Wizard** and select the fields **Crime Ref No**, **Surname**, **First Name**, **Town**, **Postcode**, **Date of Birth**, **Crime Reported** and **Location**.

     3.   Click **Next**.

Grouping levels enable the selection to be sorted. It will display a similar result to a sort within a sort if more than one field is selected.

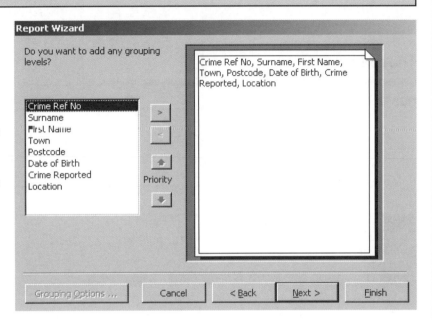

Click on the fields that you wish to group and click the selector button.

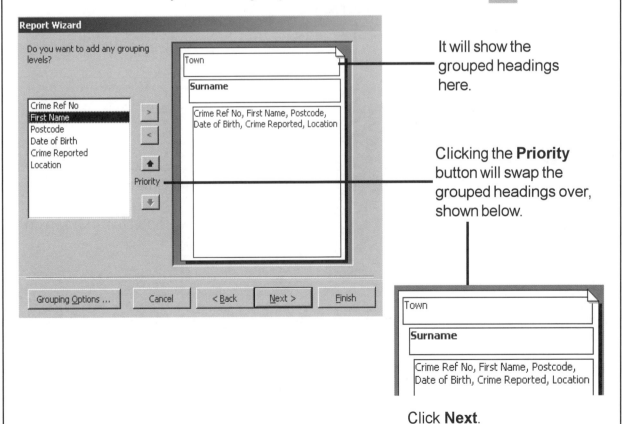

It will show the grouped headings here.

Clicking the **Priority** button will swap the grouped headings over, shown below.

Click **Next**.

The fields not selected in the grouping levels can be further sorted by clicking on the drop-down box and selecting the required field heading.

The sort order can be selected once the heading has been selected.

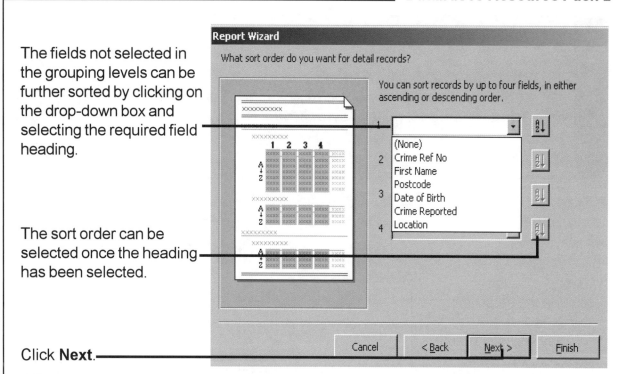

Click **Next**.

T A S K

4.   Group the **Town** field first followed by the **Surname** field.   Click **Next**.

5.   Sort the **First Name** field.   Click **Next**.

Select the **Layout** style that you require.

An example layout will appear.

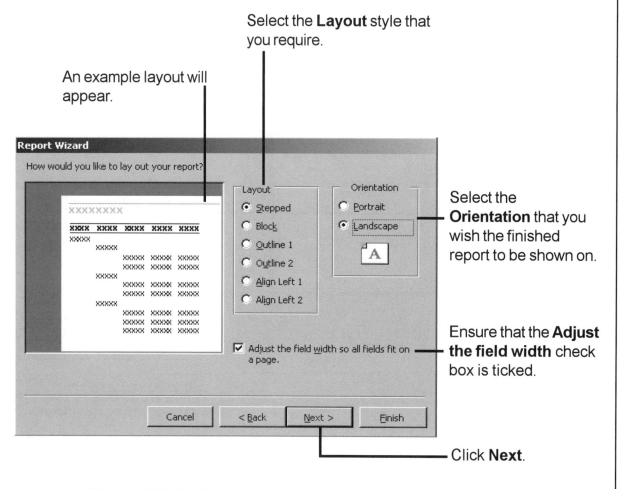

Select the **Orientation** that you wish the finished report to be shown on.

Ensure that the **Adjust the field width** check box is ticked.

Click **Next**.

T A S K

6. *Select the stepped layout style.*

7. *Set the orientation to landscape.*

8. *Make sure the **Check** box is ticked.*

9. *Click **Next.***

Select the style that you wish the text to be displayed in.

An example of the style will be shown.

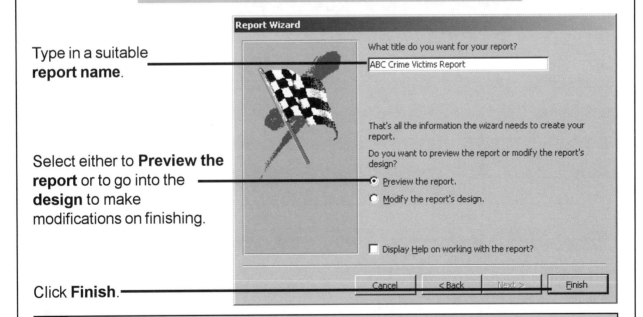

Click **Next**.

Type in a suitable **report name**.

Select either to **Preview the report** or to go into the **design** to make modifications on finishing.

Click **Finish**.

T A S K

10. *Select the bold style for the report. Click **Next**.*

11. *Name the report **ABC Crime Victims Report**. Click **Finish**.*

12. *View the finished report and close.*

The finished report will be displayed on your screen, similar to that shown below:

ABC Crime Victims Report

Town	Surname	First Name	Crime Ref No	Postcode	te of Birth	Crime Reported	Location
Bath							
	Bailey						
		Samantha	GT-2233-2B	BA5 6SE	21/11/1955	Garden Furniture Stolen	Mangotsfield
	Williams						
		Paula	MP-7894-4M	BA5 8SE	26/09/1967	Mobile Theft	Blagdon
Bristol							
	Burton						
		Emma	BT-8945-3B	BS17 2S	12/12/1981	Bike Theft	Stoke Gifford
	Dury						
		David	MG-8754-2M	BS11 9NE	14/07/1980	Mugging	Staplehill
	Graham						
		Martin	BT-8999-3B	BS12 8N	05/03/1979	Bike Theft	Filton
	Grant						
		John	CC-4455-5C	BS16 9S	14/02/1965	Credit Cards Stolen	Almondsbury
	Harrop						
		Nicholas	HB-6548-2B	BS14 2NE	24/10/1969	House Break-in	Coalpit Heath
	Hawkins						
		John	HB-1499-2B	BS16 5S	01/06/1951	House Burglary	Kingswood
	Jenkins						
		Barbara	CT-7788-3C	BS14 3NE	12/06/1975	Vehicle Tyres Slashed	Filton

07 November 2002   *Page 1 of 2*

By clicking on the Design view, the report can be modified in the same way as the forms.

The text and label boxes may need to be adjusted to show the contents.

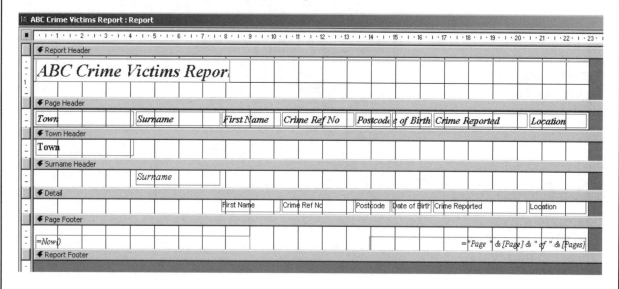

Printing A Report

Click on the **Print** icon on the toolbar.

**T
A
S
K**

1. Use the **Report Wizard** to create a report from the **ABC Police Reports Table**.

2. Use only the **Crime Ref No**, **Crime Reported**, **Location**, **Visit Required** and **Date and Time Reported** fields.

3. Group the layout on the **Crime Reported** field.

4. Sort the layout in ascending order by location.

5. Use a layout of your choice. Set to landscape and adjust the field widths to fit the page.

6. Choose any style.

7. Save the report as **ABC Crime Location Report**.

8. Print the report.

9. Close the database.

Modifying Reports

Forms and reports are made up of a series of **Controls**. Everything you add to a form or report is a control. Text boxes and label boxes are examples of controls. In Design view, the controls can be added, modified or the properties changed. Each control has its own properties; these vary depending on which type of control has been selected.

Moving and resizing modifies the report or form to display the results in an effective manner. Modifying the properties can also change the resulting display.

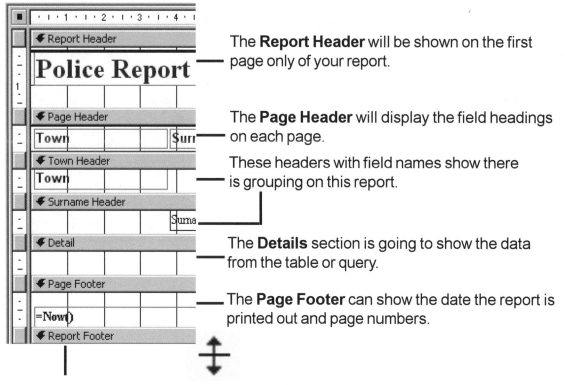

The **Report Header** will be shown on the first page only of your report.

The **Page Header** will display the field headings on each page.

These headers with field names show there is grouping on this report.

The **Details** section is going to show the data from the table or query.

The **Page Footer** can show the date the report is printed out and page numbers.

The **Report Footer** will need to be stretched by using the double-headed arrows. This is where the totalling details will be placed. It will ensure the totals are on the final page of the report.

It may be required to create a report where data is calculated, such as totalling salary bills. This is easily achieved using a report and modifying it slightly.

Functions are used to calculate specific information.

= SUM	To add the values together contained in a field
= COUNT	To count the number of values in a field
= AVG	To calculate the average of values in a field

Totalling The Report

In the **Report Footer**, draw a text box by using the **Text Box** button. This button creates a label box as well as an associated text box.

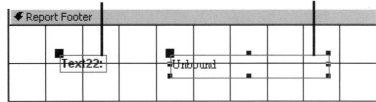

Type in the label box the name that you require.

Click in the text box and replace the word 'Unbound' with something more meaningful. We need to tell the computer which field to total.

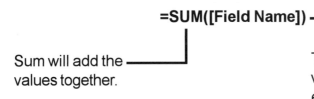

=SUM([Field Name])

Sum will add the values together.

The square brackets (**[ ]**) around a word/words indicates that the element is the name of a table, query, form, report or field.

The round brackets (**( )**) are necessary to indicate that the word **SUM** is the name of a function.

In effect, the above function will sum the particular named field contained within the brackets.

To accept the function, press the **Enter** key.

To view the result, click on the Report view. Go to the last page; it will have totalled the field.

Country	Surname	First Name	World Ranking	Points
	Davenport	Lindsay	3	3,862
	Raymond	Lisa	19	1,180
	Seles	Monica	7	2,979
	Shaughnessy	Meghann	12	1,893
	Williams	Serena	9	2,875
	Williams	Venus	1	4,790
Uzbekistan				
	Tulyaganova	Iroda	20	1,168
Yugoslavia				
	Dokic	Jelena	8	2,974
		Total		50543

However, as you will notice, it will need to be adjusted to achieve a pleasing format. The label boxes and text boxes can be moved in the same way as when designing a form.

The report will need to be modified so that the label and text box is aligned under the field heading that it is calculating.

The result from calculating the total should follow the same format as the numbers it is calculating. Therefore, if it was a currency field, the format would need to be changed to Currency, together with the number of decimal places.

Click on the Design view.

Click on the text box in the **Report Footer**.

Click on the **Properties box** icon 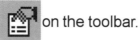 on the toolbar.

The properties box displays the underlying format.

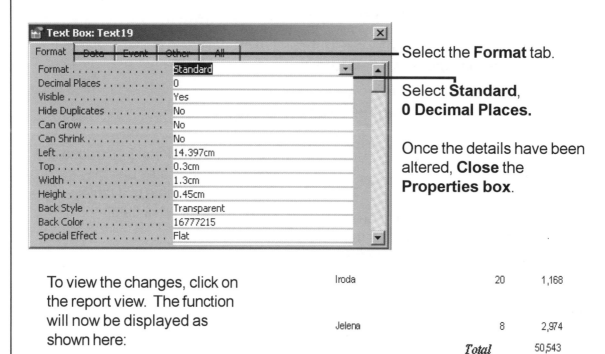

Select the **Format** tab.

Select **Standard,**
0 Decimal Places.

Once the details have been altered, **Close** the **Properties box**.

To view the changes, click on the report view. The function will now be displayed as shown here:

Iroda	20	1,168
Jelena	8	2,974
Total		50,543

TASK

1. Open the **Sports** database.

2. Create a query on the **ABC Tennis Table** to find all the **Female** tennis players. Save the query as **ABC Female Tennis Players Query**.

3. Create a report from the query **ABC Female Tennis Players Query** by using the **Report Wizard**. In the report, show only the **Surname**, **First Name**, **World Ranking**, **Country** and **Points** fields. Group by **Country**, sort by **Surname** then by **First Name**.

4. Calculate the total **Points**. Modify the report to show a visually pleasing appearance.

5. Save the report as **ABC Female Players Points Score Report**.

6. Print and close the report.

**T
A
S
K**

1. Create a query on the **Tennis** table to find all the **Male** tennis players. Save the query as **Male Tennis Players.**

2. Create a report from the query **Male Tennis Players** by using the **Report Wizard**. In the report, show only the **Surname**, **First Name**, **World Ranking**, **Country** and **Points** fields.

3. Group by **Country**, sort by **Surname** then by **First Name**.

4. Calculate the total **Points**. Modify the report to show a visually pleasing appearance.

5. Save the report as **Male Players Points Score.**

6. Print and close the report.

Ensuring Sorting And Grouping Are In Place

Once a calculation has been applied to a report, the sorting and grouping previously applied may be lost. The report can be checked simply by looking at the output data produced or:

Open the report.
Select the Design view.
Click **View** on the menu bar.
Click **Sorting and Grouping**.

> **NB** Or, instead of **View**, **Sorting and Grouping**, click on the **Sorting and Grouping** button.

The Sorting and Grouping dialogue box will appear as shown:

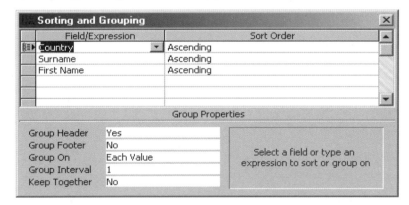

If the sorting and grouping has been lost, click on the drop-down arrow and select the field or fields required; the default sort order will be ascending.

**T
A
S
K**

1. Check that the **Country**, **Surname** and **First Name** fields still have the **Sorting and Grouping** applied in the reports **ABC Female Players Points Score Report** and **ABC Male Players Points Score Report**.

2. Save any changes made. Close the **Sports** database.

We have so far assumed that any selection of fields required in reports should be done in the Report Wizard. A more flexible approach is to create a query to prepare the data for the report and then use the Report Wizard [or Report Design View] to create the report using the query as its data source.

NB   One disadvantage of this approach is that the report doesn't always follow the sort order of the query, so you must be prepared either to repeat sorting instructions in the Report Wizard or to correct it later with the **Sorting and Grouping** tool.

T A S K	1.	*Compact the* **Police Records** *and* **Sports** *databases.*

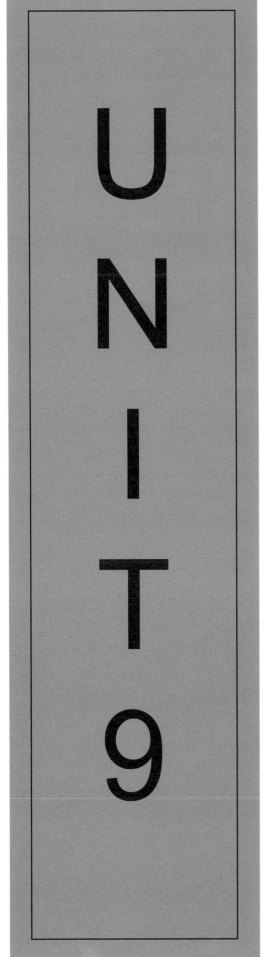

On completion of this unit, you will have learnt about and practised the following:

- **Design Properties**

  - Breakdown Of The Properties Box In The Report Design
  - Creating Label Reports
  - Changing The Record Source Property

Design Properties

Breakdown Of The Properties Box In The Report Design

Ensure you are in the Design view of a report.

Click on a text box, then on the **Properties** icon.

The text box properties dialogue box will appear.
Click the **All** tab.

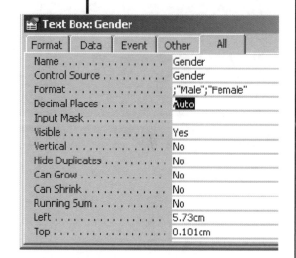

Name - is the name you gave to the text box.

Control Source - is the field the data relates to.

Format - will give you a selection, if available, dependent upon the initial design setup, eg Date/Time field will allow the same formatting properties as the table design.

Decimal Places - will allow you to specify the number of decimal places for numeric fields only.

Input Mask - will display an input mask if already specified in the table design.

Visible - default set to **Yes**. If set to **No**, the field will no longer be visible in the report view.

Hide Duplicates - will have hidden duplicated data if this had been specified earlier.

Can Grow - default is **No**. If set to **Yes**, the text box will grow in size if more data is entered.

Can Shrink - default is **No**. If set to **Yes**, the text box will decrease to fit the data entered.

Running Sum - will allow a running sum from one page to another and a final total on the last page.

The rest of the properties section allows you to change the style of the box that contains the data and the style of data, ie changing the text styles and colour and background colours and box definition etc.

You can adjust the position and formatting of report controls just as you have already practised on a form. Remember, you can use:
> The Formatting toolbar
> The **Format** page of the Properties organiser
> The Format Painter
> The alignment tools on the **Format** menu.

When you create a report using the wizard, you will often find that you will want to improve on the width and positioning of controls.

T
A
S
K

1. Open the **Sports** database.

2. Use the **AutoReport:Tabular** to create a report on the **ABC Tennis Table**.

3. The **Date of Birth**, **Play Hand** and **Gender** fields do not need to be visible. Apply a colour to the **Surname** and **First Name** field names. Apply a border width of **2pt** to the field name **Country**. Apply the font as italic to the field names **Points** and **World Ranking**.

4. View the report.

5. Save the report as **ABC Top Tennis Players Report**.

6. Print the report.

7. Close the report.

8. Close the database.

Creating Label Reports

Under **Objects**, select **Reports**. Click **New**.

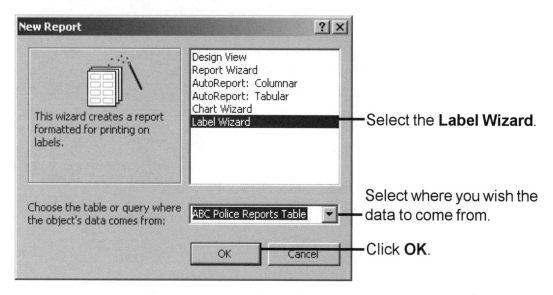

Select the **Label Wizard**.

Select where you wish the data to come from.

Click **OK**.

You will now be able to specify from the list provided the type of labels you will be using.

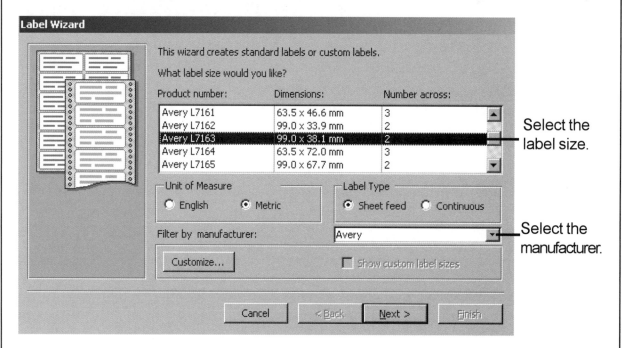

Select the label size.

Select the manufacturer.

The majority of labels will have a code number that will be referenced above. The code numbers dictate different sizes and the number of labels per sheet. The code number is found on the top and bottom of Avery labels. However, before buying a pack of labels, it is best to ensure that they are supported by the selection on your computer.

Click **Next**.

T A S K

1. *Open the **Police Records** database.*

2. *Create a **Label Report** on the **ABC Police Reports Table** using the **Label Wizard**. Use label size **Avery L7163**. Click **Next**.*

You can then specify the style of your text.

Click on the drop-down arrows and make a suitable selection.

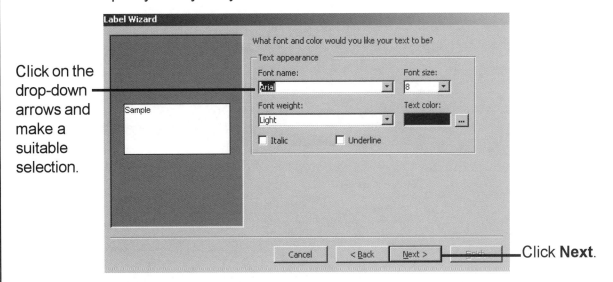

Click **Next**.

You can then specify the data that you require from the available fields.

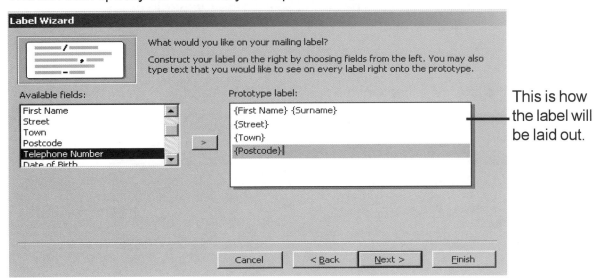

This is how the label will be laid out.

Click on the field required from the available list and click on the field selector. ❯

Press **Enter** to take you to a new line.

Select the next field required and continue until all your desired fields are in place on the prototype label.

NB Some fields such as First Names and Surnames would be better placed next to each other. To do this, select the first field, press **Spacebar** then select the second field. Press **Enter** to go to a new line. Continue as above.

Click **Next**.

T A S K

3. *Specify the style as **Arial, Normal** and size **10pt**.*

4. *Include on your label the fields **First Name**, **Surname**, **Street**, **Town** and **Postcode**. Click **Next**.*

You can now sort the labels by particular fields.

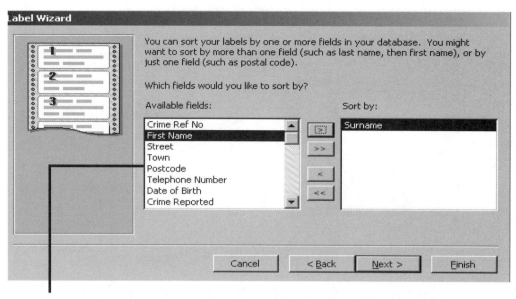

Select the field or fields required to be sorted by from the **Available fields** list. Click the field selector button.

Click **Next**.

You can give the labels a suitable name.

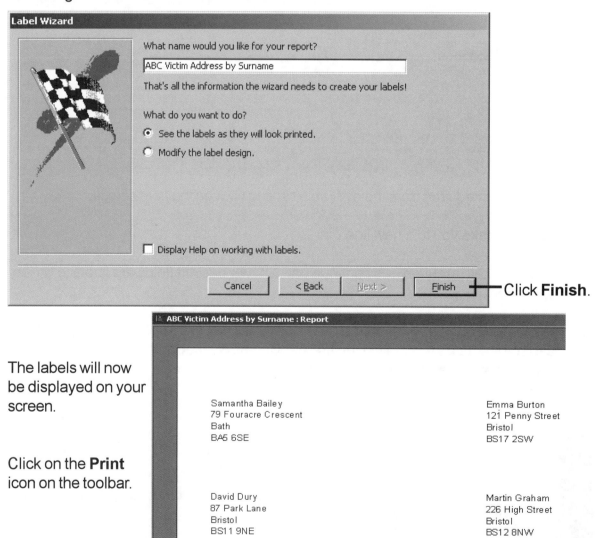

Click **Finish**.

The labels will now be displayed on your screen.

Click on the **Print** icon on the toolbar.

T A S K	5.	Sort the labels on the **Surname** field.
	6.	Save the labels with the name **ABC Victim Address by Surname**.
	7.	Print the labels on paper only.
	8.	Close the label report.

Changing The Record Source Property

This facility allows you to use the same report format but with a different sort of information, ie query or table.

Ensure you are in the Design view of the report for which you wish to change the record source.

Click **Edit**.
Click **Select Report**.

Click on the **Properties** icon on the toolbar.

Click on the **All** tab.

In the **Record Source** row, click on the drop-down arrow. This will give you all the tables and select queries created in that database.

Select the table or query where you wish the new data to be selected from.

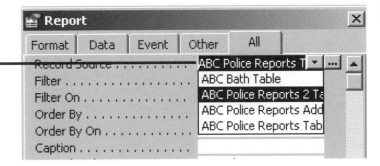

Close the **Properties** box.

Click on the report view to see the new data displayed.

T A S K	1.	Ensure you are working on the **Police Records** database.
	2.	Open the report **ABC Victim Address by Surname**. Change the **Record Source** to **ABC Police Reports 2 Table**. View the report.
	3.	Print the new report. Close and save the changes.
	4.	Compact the **Police Records** and **Sports** databases.

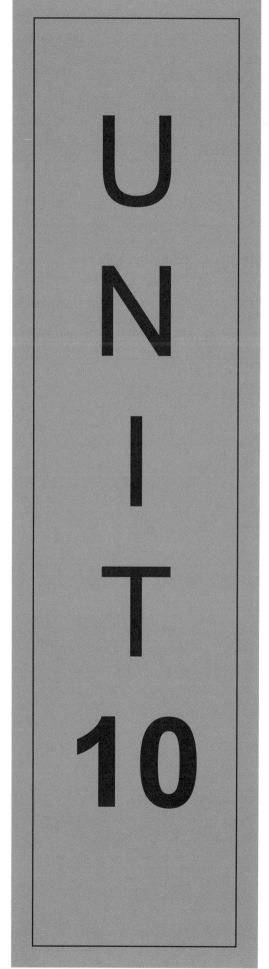

On completion of this unit, you will have learnt about and practised the following:

- **Export A Database**

- Exporting A Table From One Database To Another
- Using The Documenter
- Defining Object Types Using Documenter
- Creating A Backup Copy

Exporting A Table

Exporting A Table From One Database To Another

Exporting means that you can export any of your database objects to another Access database; you can take the table from one database and place it into another. This is effectively the same as copying and pasting objects between databases. You can export only one object at a time.

Highlight the table you want to export.

Click **File**. ——

Click **Export**. ——

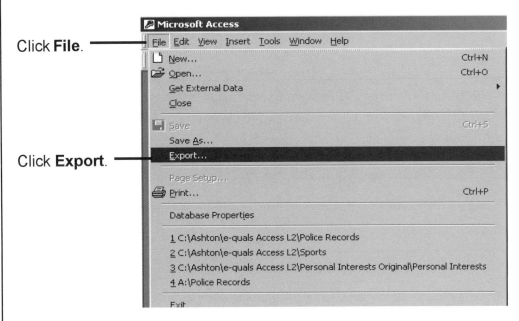

You will then need to select the database location and the new database that you wish to export the table to.

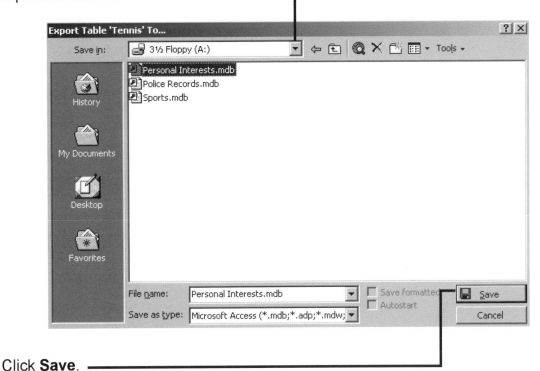

Click **Save**. ——

You can, at this stage, give the table a new name as desired.

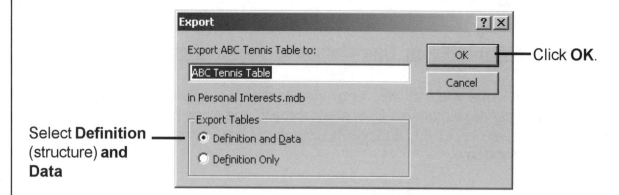

Select **Definition** (structure) **and Data**

The dialogue screens will now disappear and the table will be in its new location.

| T A S K | 1. | *Export the **ABC Tennis Table** from the **Sports** database to the **Personal Interests** database.* |
| | 2. | *Ensure the export was successful.* |

Using The Documenter

Viewing a database structure prior to entering information is considered a useful tool, allowing the user an insight into the design features, thereby increasing efficiency. The Documenter provides ease of use and printing facility.

Close any database objects before commencing.

Click **Tools**.

Click **Analyze**.

Click **Documenter**.

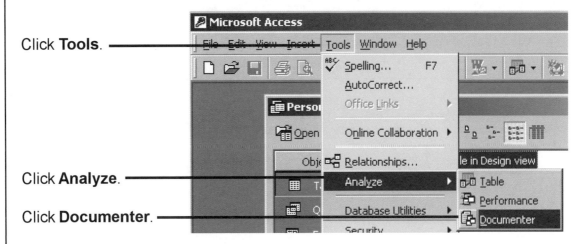

The **Documenter** dialogue box will appear (shown below).

Place a tick against the **Writers and Poets** table.

Click **Options**.

Place a tick against the **Properties** box.

Click on the radio button for **Names, Data Types and Sizes**.

Click on the radio button for **Nothing**.

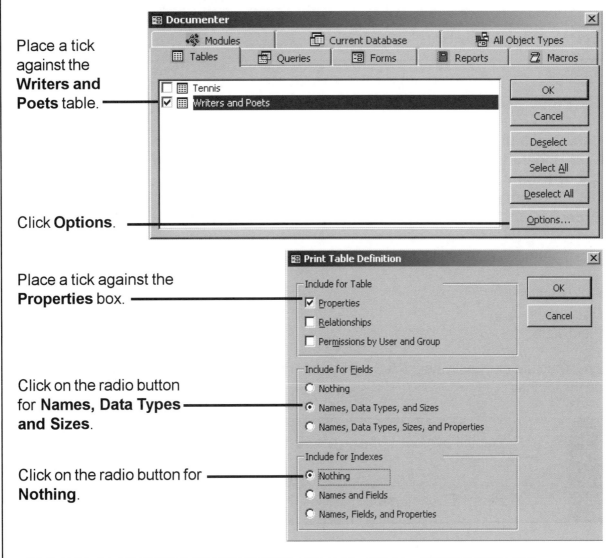

Click **OK**.

The following screen will then appear, showing the basic structure of the database.

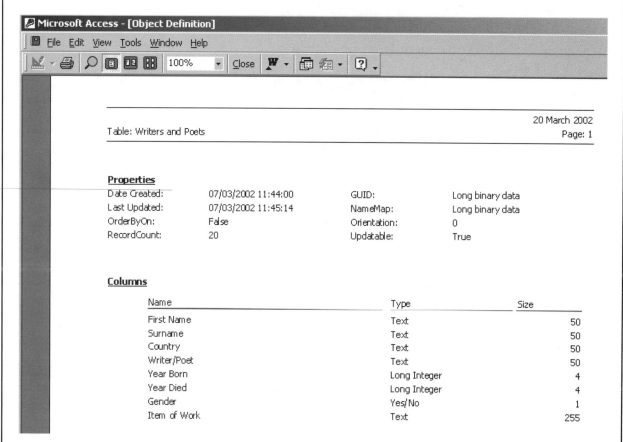

The **Properties** section displays:

Date Created:	Date and time the database was created.
Last Updated:	Date and time the database was last updated.
RecordCount:	Displays the number of records in the table.
Def. Updatable:	Displays if the table can be updated.
OrderByOn:	Displays the field name that contains a sort.

The **Columns** section displays:

Field names
Data types
Field sizes

The structure can easily be printed out by clicking on the **Print** icon on the toolbar.

T	1.	*Produce a printout of the structure for the **Writers and Poets** table using Documenter.*
A		
S		
K	2.	*Close the Documenter.*

Defining Object Types Using Documenter

Open the database and select **Tables** from **Objects**.
Select a table and right-click.

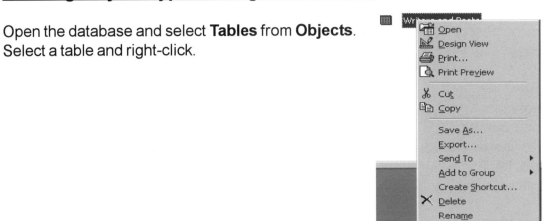

Click **Properties**. ─────────────────

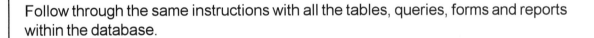

Type an appropriate description ──── about the table.

Click **Apply**.

Click **OK**.

Follow through the same instructions with all the tables, queries, forms and reports within the database.

To print the required information, follow the procedure precisely:

Click **Tools**.
Click **Analyze**.
Click **Documenter**.
Select the **Tables** tab.
Click **Select All** (selects all tables).
Click **Options**.

Tick **Properties**.

Tick **Names, Data Types, and Sizes**.

Tick **Names and Fields**.
Click **OK**.
Click **OK**.

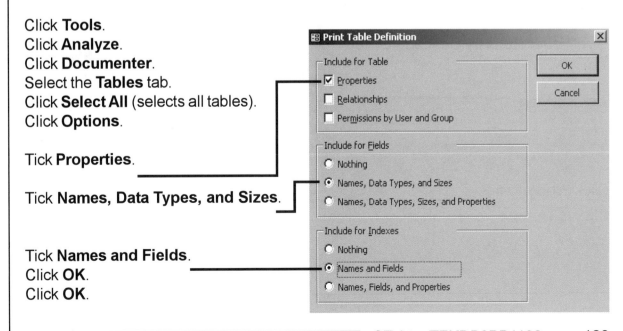

Print the Documenter on screen; this will print out the Documenter for the tables including the descriptions typed. Each object will be printed on a separate page.

Click **Tools**.
Click **Analyze**.
Click **Documenter**.
Select the **Queries** tab.
Click **Select All**.
Click **Options**.

Tick **Properties**.

Tick **Names, Data Types, and Sizes**.

Tick **Names and Fields**.

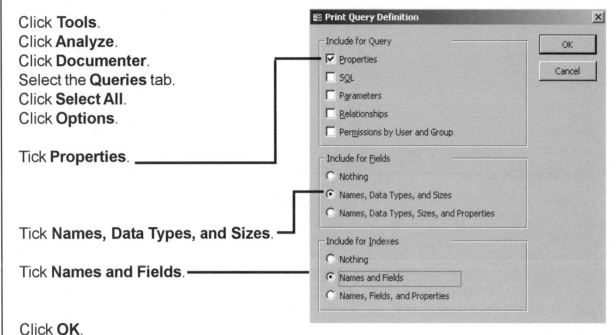

Click **OK**.
Click **OK**.

Print the Documenter on screen; this will print out the Documenter for the queries, including the descriptions typed. Each object will be printed on a separate page.

Click **Tools**.
Click **Analyze**.
Click **Documenter**.
Select the **Forms** tab.
Click **Select All**.
Click **Options**.

Tick **Properties**.

Tick **Permissions by User and Group**.

Tick **Nothing**.

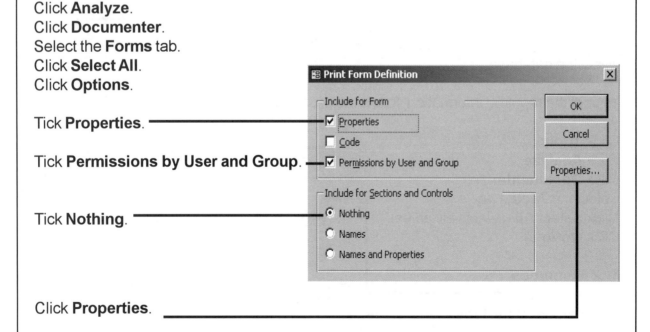

Click **Properties**.

Ensure there is an **x** against **Other Properties**.

Unselect all the others.

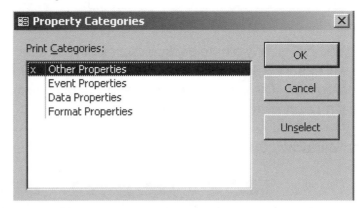

Click **OK**.
Click **OK**.
Click **OK**.

Print the Documenter on screen; this will print out the Documenter for the forms including the descriptions typed. Each object will be printed on a separate page.

To use the Documenter for reports, follow through the same instructions as for forms, but select the **Reports** tab.

T **A** **S** **K**	1.	*Use the **Documenter** to view the printouts that would result when the details of the object types for the **Police Records** database are viewed in print preview.*
	2.	*A printout of the **Documenter** is **NOT** required at present.*

Creating A Backup Copy

You should regularly create backup copies of your data onto a separate storage medium. This will ensure data is recoverable if the system crashes or the original file is deleted or tampered with. The following screens and instructions may differ slightly depending on the operating environment that you are using.

Open **Windows Explorer**.

Click **3¹/₂ Floppy A:** ————

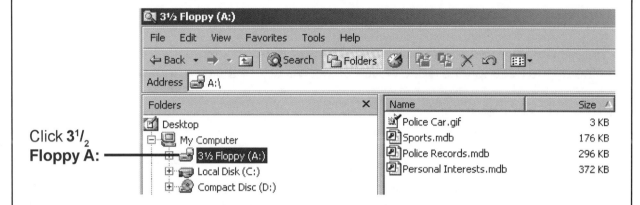

Click **File**.
Click **New**.
Click **Folder**.

Type in **Personal Interests Original** as the folder name. ————

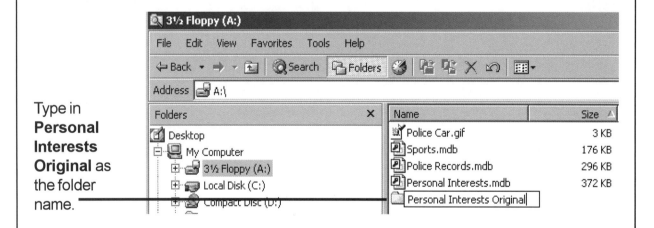

Press the **Enter** key to agree the folder name.

Select the **Personal Interests** database.

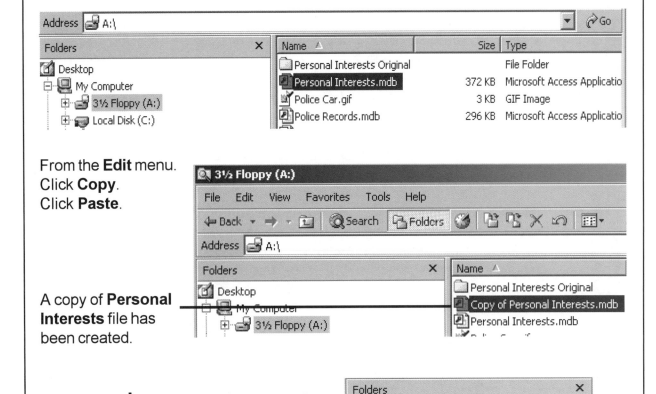

From the **Edit** menu.
Click **Copy**.
Click **Paste**.

A copy of **Personal Interests** file has been created.

Click on the **+** next to the **3¹/₂ Floppy A:** this will view the folder on the left side of your screen.

Click and drag the **Copy of Personal Interests** file into the **Personal Interests Original** folder on the left side of the screen.

T A S K	1.	Create a folder called **Personal Interests Original** folder on your floppy disk. Create a backup copy of the **Personal Interests** database and place it in the **Personal Interests Original** folder.
	2.	Close **Windows Explorer**.

CONSOLIDATION EXERCISE

1. Delete the databases on your floppy disk - this can be done using Windows Explorer. Select the databases and press the **Delete** key on the keyboard. Confirm deletion.

2. Locate the database called **Paperback Thrills** from the network. Copy the database to your floppy disk.

3. Open the **Paperback Thrills** database and view the contents.

4. Create a query which includes all fields apart from **ID** and which sorts the books in order of their publication dates, the most recent coming first. Call it **ABC Books Query**. Close the query.

5. Create a form in Design view, using **ABC Books Query** as your record source and showing all fields. Select a 12pt font of your choice for the labels and another 12pt font for the text boxes.
Use the **Format** page of the Properties organiser to change the height of all your controls to 0.6cm and the width to 4cm. The title box will require stretching to fit the contents. Use the alignment tools to arrange your form neatly. Save with the name **ABC Books Form**.

Create a Form Header saying **Paperback Thrills**. Format the font as a larger version of your label font. Adjust the size and position of the label to suit. Save the changes and close.

6. Open the **Books Table** in Design view. After the **Title** field, insert a field called **Notes** - the data type should be **Memo**. Save and close.

7. Open the query in Design view and add the **Notes** field.
Move the **Notes** field so that it is positioned after the **Title** field. To move a field within a query, select the field by clicking on the field selector (grey bar just above the field name).

Title	Publisher	Date	Pages	Price	Notes	
Books Table	Books Table	Books Table	Books Table	Books Table	Books Table	
		Descending				
☑	☑	☑	☑	☑	☑	

Click and drag to the new position (a thick black bar will indicate where the field will be displayed). Select Datasheet view to view the changes. Save the changes and close the query.

8. Open the **ABC Books Form** in Design view. Use the Field List to place your Notes field either beside the Title field or just below it (you may need to move other controls out of the way to do this). Use the Properties organiser to give its label the same height and width as the other labels. Adjust the height and width of your Notes text box so that it will accommodate at least two lines of writing. Rearrange and realign your controls to look neat.

CONSOLIDATION EXERCISE CONTINUED

9. On the **ABC Books Form**, change the tab order so that your new field comes after **Title**. Save the changes.

10. In Form view, add the following new data as records:

Forename	James	Stephen	J.D.
Surname	Patterson	King	Robb
Title	The Beach House	Black House	Purity in Death
Notes	Joint author with Peter de Jonge	Joint author with Peter Straub	Joint author with Nora Roberts
Publisher	Headline	HarperCollins	Berkley
Date	22.7.02	2.9.02	1.9.02
Pages	294	819	384
Price	£10.99	£6.99	£7.99

NB **When you want to leave a Memo field, pressing the Enter key doesn't work – Access thinks you want to begin a new line in the field. You have to use Tab or the arrow keys.**

11. Scroll through the records and observe that your three new records are all at the end, ie not in date order. Close the form and open it again. This has made the query run afresh so the sort order has been corrected – your new records are now in the right place.

12. Close the form and open the table. Notice that, although the **ID** field wasn't on your form, Access has supplied the ID numbers. (Users don't often want to see ID numbers – it's Access that needs them.) Close the table.

13. Open the **ABC Books Form** in Design view. Place a Clip Art image of a book next to your title in the Form Header.

    Click in the Form Header Section.
    Select **Insert, Object** from the menu bar.
    Select **Microsoft Clip Gallery**.
    Click **OK**.
    Type **book** in the **Search for clips** box and press Return.
    Select an image by clicking on it, select **Insert Clip** from the pop-up menu.
    Close the **Clip Art Gallery** dialogue box.
    Move the picture so that it appears to the right of the heading. Resize the picture so that it is 2 or 3 times the height of your heading.
    Open the Properties organiser of the image and change the **Size Mode** to **Zoom** (this sizes the image to the size of the box - so that all the image is viewable). You may now need to reduce the size of the Form Header.

CONSOLIDATION EXERCISE CONTINUED

14. Add suitable commands to your form using the **Control Wizards** button in the Toolbox. Ensure the commands work and save the changes. Close the form.

15. Open the **Books Table** in Datasheet view. Penguin have bought up Black Swan (this and all the other developments in these tasks are make-believe). Use the **Find and Replace** tool to find the mention of Black Swan and replace it with **Penguin**.

16. James Patterson has been involved in a legal dispute and Headline are withdrawing his books. Use the Find tool to find the first record containing his name, close the Find tool and delete the record. Keep repeating this routine until you have deleted all of his records.

17. An Orion agent calls and wants to know which of her books are on your list. Create a query which displays all fields apart from **ID** and restricts the publisher to **Orion**. Check that the query works. Change the query to make it a make-table query to create a table called **ABC Orion Table**. Run the query. Save the query as **ABC Orion Table Query**. Check that the new table has the records you expect.

18. HarperCollins are taking over Orion and you want your Orion table to show HarperCollins books as well. Create a query based on the **Books Table** to show all fields apart from **ID**, publisher being restricted to HarperCollins. Look at its Datasheet view to check that it works. In Design view, change it into an append query to append records to the **ABC Orion Table**. Run the query, save it as **ABC HarperCollins Query** and check its results in the table.

19. Penguin are increasing their basic paperback price to £7.99. Create a query on the **Books Table** with only the **Publisher** and **Price** fields, restricting the publisher to Penguin. Check that it's working. In Design view, change the query to an Update Query and set the **Price** field to update to £7.99. Save it as **ABC Penguin Increase Query**. Run the query and check its results in the table.

20. Arrow publishers have gone out of business. You need to delete their books from your database. Create a query with all the fields of the **Books Table**, with the publisher confined to Arrow. Make the query into a delete query and save it as **ABC Lost Arrow Query**. Run the query and check its results in the table.

21. Create a query on the **Books Table**, showing all fields and sorting the data in ascending order of price followed by ascending order of number of pages. Save as **ABC Value Query** – it will let you see which books give the greatest number of pages in each price category.

C O N S O L I D A T I O N   E X E R C I S E   C O N T I N U E D

22. Create a query on **Books Table**, using all the fields of records which have an entry in the **Notes** field. Call it **ABC Notes Query**.

23. Create a query which lists all fields of the **Books Table** which cost at least £10 or which have at least 500 pages. Call it **ABC Big Books Query**.

24. Close any open queries or tables.

25. Create a report on the **Books Table** using the Report Wizard. Show the Forename, Surname, Title and Publisher fields. Group on Publisher and sort by Surname and Title. Name the report as **ABC Wizard Report**.

26. Now produce a similar report but only showing the records for Orion and HarperCollins books. First, create a query, **ABC Orion Plus Query**, to show the same four fields, with Publisher restricted to Orion or HarperCollins. Check that the query works. Then create a report using the Report Wizard, based on that query. Sorting and grouping as before. Name the report as **ABC Query Report**.

27. Close the database.

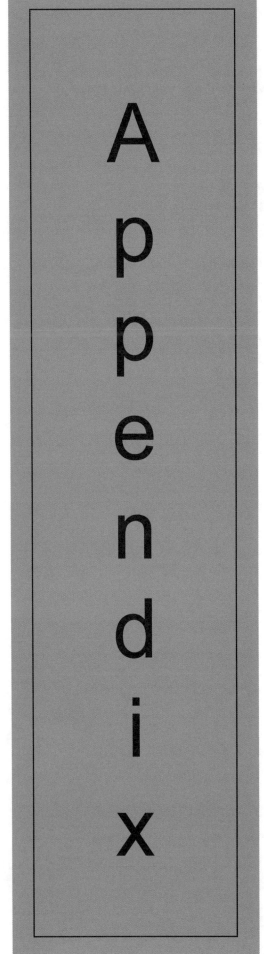

The Appendix covers:

- Glossary Of Terms
- Microsoft Access Shortcut Keys

Glossary Of Terms

Action query	A query that copies or changes data.
Advanced Filter/ Sort window	A window with which you can create a filter from scratch. You can also specify a sort order.
Append query	An action query that adds the records in a queries result set to the end of an existing table.
Column	A vertical stack, showing the value of a field in every record.
Column selector	A horizontal bar at the top of a column that you click to select an entire column.
Control	A graphical object, such as a text box or check box, that you place on a form or report in a Design view are all known as controls.
Current record	The record in a recordset that you can modify or retrieve data from. Only one record from a recordset can be the current record.
Data type	The attribute of a variable or field that determines what kind of data it can hold.
Database	A collection of data and objects related to a particular topic or purpose.
Database objects	Tables, queries, forms, reports, macros and modules.
Database window	The window that appears when you open Access.
Default value	A value that is automatically entered into a field or control.
Design view	A window in which you can create new database objects and modify existing ones.
Expression	Any combination of operators, functions, field names and properties that evaluates to a single value.
Field	An element of a table that contains a specific item of information.
Filter	A set of criteria applied to records in order to show a subset of records.
Form	An Access object used for entering data.
Format	Specifies how numbers, dates etc are to be displayed.

Index	A reference to a table that Microsoft Access can use to locate records more rapidly.
Input mask	A format you specify to assist with data entry into a control or field.
Label	A control that contains descriptive text, such as a title.
Menu bar	The first set of menu choices to appear on the top line of the screen at the beginning of an Access session.
Null	A value that appears missing or unknown data.
Preview	To view data or modules that will appear on screen as they will be printed.
Query	A question you ask about the data stored in Access tables.
Record	Each row of an Access table. Each record is a group of related information.
Recordset	The collective name given to tables.
Report	Information from tables, forms or queries presented in the required format.
Select query	A query that asks a question from the data stored in the table and returns a result set.
Separator	A character that separates text or numbers.
Sort order	The order in which records are displayed.
Table	A structure made up of rows (records) and columns (fields) that contain related information.
Table properties	Attributes of a table that affect the appearance or behaviour of the table as a whole.
Toolbox	The sets of tools that you use in Design view to place controls on a form or report.
Validation rule	A rule that sets limits and conditions on what can be entered into one or more fields.
Value	The text or date etc that completes a condition that a field must meet for searching or filtering.
Wizard	An Access tool which takes you through specific functions, ie building a query, building a report etc.

Microsoft Access Shortcut Keys

By pressing the key or combination of keys, the software will do the following:

F1	Displays the Office Assistant.
F2	Switches to editing mode.
F3	To find the next occurrence of the text specified in the **Find** or **Replace** dialogue box.
F4	To open a combo box.
F5	Switching between Form view and Form design.
F6	Switch between upper and lower portions of a window.
F7	To check spelling.
F8	To utilise extend mode.
F9	To refresh the contents of a combo box.
F10	To make the menu bar active.
F11	To bring the Database window to the front.
F12	To open the **Save As** dialogue box.
Ctrl+N	Opens a new database.
Ctrl+O	Opens an existing database.
Ctrl+P	To print the current or selected object.
Ctrl+S	To save database object.
Ctrl+R	To select a form or report.
Ctrl+W	To close the active window.
Ctrl+C	To copy the selection.
Ctrl+X	To cut the selection.
Ctrl+V	To paste the selection.
Ctrl+Z	Undo typing.

This is not an exhaustive list.

This Page is

intentionally

Left Blank

This Page is intentionally Left Blank

This Page is

intentionally

Left Blank